Australian Legends

C. W. Peck

Australian Legends

Copyright © 2019 Indo-European Publishing

The present edition is a reproduction of previous publication of this classic work. Minor typographical errors may have been corrected without note, however, for an authentic reading experience the spelling, punctuation, and capitalization have been retained from the original text.

ISBN: 978-1-64439-100-6

CONTENTS

PRELUDE: A PRINCESS

In a little settlement for aborigines not far from Sydney lives the last full-blooded person of the once-powerful Cammary Tribe. She lives in the past. The present has no lure for her, and very little interest.

She has to eat and she has to sleep and she has to dress.

She looks for no pleasure, but she finds pleasure in the thoughts she has of her earliest childhood, and the knowledge she has of the real South Coast aborigine.

She is a princess, and she is also the sister-in-law of the man who was the last king of his group.

Both groups were of the one tribe, and each group had its king.

She has the true aboriginal cast of countenance, and she speaks most fluently to those who can understand or only partly understand the language of her people.

And her people are of two groups, for she said to the writer, "My mother was of the North; my father was of the South; I speak between the two!"

And her English is of a pleasing kind, for it is not in any sense "pidgin." It is soft in accent and musical in tone.

She does not know her age, for, as she puts it, "I did not go to school."

She knew many beautiful legends.

But they have nearly all gone from her, for she never told them. She heard them and forgets nearly all. She hears no more, for they are seldom spoken of by the remnant of her race.

Time was when the story-teller was an honoured man, when he dressed for his part, when the young people were educated in the lore of the land and the law of the land, by means of legend.

But there is so much white blood in the people that practically none wish to bear the stories of the "Alcheringa," and so the stories have faded.

But not all.

And the religious beliefs!

They are still very real to this "Last of Her Tribe."

Just as real as ours are to us.

"Don't think that the white man told us about God," said Ellen.

"My people always knew about Him. Their fathers told them. Our God was never a wooden idol, nor a thing carved by human hands. He was always up in the Heavens where He lived, and from where He looked down upon all the world, and sought out the evil doers and punished them in many ways. From His throne He caused by His will the food to come upon the trees and the game to add to the larder. And He made the rain to fall, and He shook the earth with His thunder, and He threatened with the lightning! And there were good men who could see Him and get Him to move!"

So said Ellen.

To pray to Him was the most natural thing for the people to do, and there were those whose principal mission it was to do that. They were the good men-the Clergymen, the Priests.

He made it the duty, too, of the people to inflict punishment upon the wrong doers that were caught and proved to be malefactors. Therefore it was, that men were sometimes stood up and speared, and women were beaten with nullahs.

There were the doctors, also. These men gave much time to the study and practice of the healing art, and sorcery and witchery did not escape their especial notice-just as the white people have their crystal readers and fortune-tellers to-day right in all our capital cities.

The doctors knew much of the effect of the eating of herbs and the drinking of water in which herbs had been steeped. They provided the leaves and the bark that were thrown into the water-holes in order to stupefy fish, as well as the medicines for the cure of the ills of the people. In their sorcery they played upon the emotions just as our mesmerists and evangelists do.

All this the old Princess of the aboriginal settlement tells, but not to everyone. Only to those who have a sympathy and an understanding, and a readable wish to learn the deeper things of the aboriginal mind.

There is, in a gully near Appin, a place that was sacred for, possibly, many thousands of years.

The gully is deep, and the head of it is a big round water-hole with precipitous sides, ever one of which the water pours in a roaring, tumbling, spraying fall.

The fall is governed now by the gates and spillways of the

Cataract Dam, but until that was built it was governed only by the rains that fell and the winds that blew.

And the way down to the pool was always difficult.

None but the priest ever descended there, and when he did he carried with him the flint rod that served as the bell in the church steeple of the white man does-to call-but with the difference that the bell calls the people, and the flint called the gods or the spirits.

Tap, tap, tap, tap went the flint on the sandstone, and ages of tapping wore a hole that is not even seen by the great majority that clamber there now, much less understood.

My Black Princess heard of that Sacred Place when she was a tiny child.

She has never been to Appin, but her father and other great men of her group have been there and they told of the Sacred Spot when they returned to the coast.

It was a church, and nothing else, yet built, not with hands, but by the will of the God that the aborigines knew.

Our name for the Princess is Ellen, and Ellen's eyes glowed when she told the writer of her God.

And how they glowed when the writer told Ellen of the Sacred Spot near Appin, and when he showed that he knew the meaning of the worn hole and the ages of tapping!

"The place is 'kulkul,'" said Ellen, "and 'kurringaline,' and yet it is not 'pourangiling.' No 'kurru' are there!"

A ROYAL VISIT

My office was very small, and very stuffy, though under the floor covering whenever I lifted it up, it was damp and mildewed.

The day was hot and steamy, and before me on the desk was a loose-leaf ledger that simply bristled and screamed with figures.

The headings were such as this: "30 x 5.77 Covers, 710 x 90 Covers, 30 x 31 B.E. Covers, many-figured Tubes," etc., etc., and the columns were serial numbers of tyres containing as many as nine figures.

One figure denoted the year in which the tyres were manufactured, another the month, and intervening figures accounted for wealth of fabric or cord, and other details of tyre-building.

For we were distributors of motor-tyres.

The little half-door between me and the shop gave me a view of the counter; and the shelves, packed with little red bags, were heavy with their goods.

In the little red bags were the inner tubes.

Men came in and went out.

Some took price-lists. Some asked questions only, and then retired.

Some made a purchase and haggled about the discount, and some wanted to see the Chief.

My eyes ached and my head was not altogether free from a feeling like neuralgia.

The mildew, the heat, the figures-all were contributing factors.

Then I heard a voice that made me drop my pen and peer out towards that end of the counter near the door, and just out of my view as I remained seated and at ease.

As near to the outside door as she could stand while yet within the shop-that is the position taken up by the owner of the voice.

And such a voice! Smooth and soft and cushioned!

As velvet is soft to the touch, so this voice is soft to the ear. Perhaps not everyone's ear, but certainly to mine.

4

My twisting office-chair creaked as I stood up. Stood up to attention as rigidly-hatless and coatless as I was-just as I sprang to it with a click when the General addressed me away over in Palestine.

"Nungurra ilukka," I said.

The owner of the voice-a lady-shy, timid, reserved, refined-turned to me.

"That is the language of my people," she said.

"Come here, please, and speak to me," I said.

Now I have heard some people snigger at the walk of those to whom this lady belonged.

It is certainly as different from that of most Sydney people, or any other white people, as the step of a peacock is from the tramp of a camel. It has the qualities of the peacock.

It is soft. It is noiseless. It is dainty.

It takes up its full share of the floor. Every toe finds its level, and the heel is planted as firmly as the supports of the Sydney Harbour Bridge.

As I said before, it is noiseless.

When I had found the lady a seat, and had resumed mine, I asked, "In what part of your country were you born?"

She answered evasively.

It is as natural for her and her people to be evasive as it is for the most shrewd of us to refrain from telling the whole truth when we want to sell a secondhand car or a groggy horse.

"My father," she said, "came from the South and my mother from the North. His language was not the same as my mother's. I speak between the two. My words are both his and hers. Yours are neither. You speak like the people of far, far away. I do not understand you. But I know your words are of my country."

Then she leaned forward and put a hand as soft as her footfall and as soft as her voice, on my shoulder.

She peered into my face and searched me as if she expected to see something she would be afraid of.

But she was not afraid.

"Excuse me putting my hand on your shoulder," she said. "Perhaps I have no right to do it. But I know now you do not mind, and you will understand."

Then her lips quivered and her eyes filled.

She leaned forward.

"You know my people?"

She questioned me.

Yet it was not really a question. It was a statement of fact.

5

"Yes," I said, "I know your people!"

Then she overflowed.

"And aren't they GOOD people?"

It was an unburdening! It was a cry!

"Yes," I said. "They ARE good people!"

Then she removed her hat.

Her hair is white and old.

"My father was a King. I am a Princess. My blood is royal!"

"And where was your father a King?"

"He was a King of his people, and they lived around Wollongong. I am a native of the Wollongong district-born at Unanderra!"

"Was your father ever crowned?" I asked.

"Yes," she said, "when I was a grown girl-a young woman-he was crowned by the white people at a Wollongong Show. They gave him the title of 'King Mickey!'"

Then I saw a picture of my tiny boyhood.

In the Show ring, just after the high-jumping contest was decided, a black man was taken by the hand by a Wollongong dignitary and led to a small dais.

Some ceremony was enacted, but I was too small and too young to understand.

I saw that black man invested with something, and the people cheered and the black man shouted and waved his hands, and he had a string round his neck, and a brass crescent hung over his broad hairy chest.

"I saw your father crowned," I said, "and since then I have seen many of your people. They are GOOD people."

I bowed my royal visitor out.

She carried an inscribed copy of a little book about her folk.

"My grandchildren will read it to me," she said, "and I will come back one day, and I will tell you some more of our stories-stories we do not tell excepting to our own people. But I will tell them to you!"

"This," I said, "is a Royal visit."

She paused.

"Your people came here and took our country," she said very quietly, "but just a few of you understand us. I go now to Wollongong." My Royal visitor has been back to my office.

6

THE FIRST WARATAH

Why did the early arrivals in Australia imagine that the aborigines had no folk-lore, no legends, hardly any manners, habits and customs? Is it that they really had none, or that the blacks were merely incomprehensible? I think it was the latter.

Australia had much of country to be explored difficult country-on the Coast cool and equable of climate, on the highlands rough, jagged, and cold, on the Great Plains desert, with all the heat and madness of a great gravelled and sandy waste and the tales that may be told, known and unknown, are tales of endurance and adventure, rivalling truth and fiction of the sixteenth century.

One of the prettiest is the true story of Barrallier and its sequel. Barrallier carved his name on a gum-tree in one of the roughest of the foothills of the Great Dividing Range in 1802.

He was an officer in the Navy. He was fired with a desire to explore. But he was thwarted by his officers-the Commander refused him leave. Then did the Governor show that resource that is now supposed to be possessed solely by the Australian Digger.

The Digger, being British, but inherited it; and if the Tommy generally is without it, it is because Tommy generally is not Tommy specially.

Governor King learned of Barrellier's great desire, and as Governor King could make appointments irrespective of the naval commander, he gave Lieutenant Barrallier, R.N., the post of aide to himself. And then Governor Philip Gidley King, also R.N., sent his aide on an embassy to a mythical King of the Burragorang Tribe, away in those rocky fastnesses in the foothills of Australia's Great Dividing Range. Barrallier got down into that now far-famed Valley, and we, who do it in cars on a road blasted out of the side of a sheer precipice two thousand feet deep, wonder how!

There really was a king down there, and his name was Camoola. He was polite and eager to assist, if withal curious. He led Barrallier over a trackless defile, and showed the way up the rock walls by the track of the bush rat or the dingo.

But he developed a will to elbow Barrallier down into the ravine again.

No protestations availed to cause Camoola to continue in the direction Barrallier's compass pointed as the way to the interior. The white man grew angry; Camoola grew sullen. Camoola tried to tell something, even brandishing a spear, and Barrallier thought that demonstration a menace. Barrallier showed his teeth, and that night he was deserted. Sunrise showed that Camoola and his dusky satellites had vanished. The pointing of the spear was to illustrate that should the journey be continued another tribe's country would be trespassed upon, and war would be the result.

And Barrallier was in the thick gullied bush, surrounded by great forbidding walls of rock, and there grew the lovely Prostanthera[1] with it, purple baby-toothed flowers, the wild Clematis, the beautiful Araucaria, the laurel-like Rapanea[2] variabilis, the Alsophila excelsa, the myrtles, and that glorious plant and flower that to-day is the pride of every Australian who sees it and knows its history, and knows the fact that of all the world only Australia and Tasmania have it-have its whole genus-the WARATAH!

Its genus name was given to it by the great botanist Brown, and that was after it had been wrongly described as an Embothrium.

In 1818 Brown named the genus-which comprises three varieties-Telopea, because it is seen from afar; Queensland's waratah is Telopewa speciosissima; that variety also grows in South Wales, as also does Victoria's, which is called Telopea oredes, and the little beauty, the joy of the artist, is Tasmania's Telopea truncata.

But this little bit of botany is a digression.

Barrallier got out, and after reporting adversely of his black guides, he was returned to the navy, and his end came to him back in his native England, after being entrusted by the British Government with the task of erecting Cleopatra's Needle on the Thames Embankment.

Though he did not know it, we revere the name of Barrallier, and we glory in the deeds that were his. At the top of a rocky pass is his name cut in a giant gum-tree, and the date "1802."

Now for the sequel.

Many months afterwards a fine specimen of the Burragorang tribe found his way to a settler's house not far from Parramatta. He

---

[1] Prostanthera, the white variety of Tasmania is known as snow-flower.
[2] Rapanea variabilis, a laurel,--Alsophila, a tree tern; Araucaria cunninghami, a pine tree; Embothrium, a family of red ftwering plants in South America.

was none other than Camoola. And strange as it may seem, Camoola had had tidings brought him of Barrallier's adverse report. Two Hunter River blacks who were with Barrallier had returned to the Burragorang Valley with the story, and they taught to Camoola a little of the white man's tongue. He bore as a peace offering the national flower of his race-the only flower that the black man ever plucked to show a white man-the waratah.

And Camoola told its story.

Long years ago there lived a beautiful aboriginal maiden named Krubi. She had made for herself a cloak of the red skin of the rock wallaby, and she had ornamented it with the redder crests of the gang-gang cockatoo. It was said down in the Burragorang Valley to be the only cloak of its kind in the world. And Krubi knew of a man who was far enough removed in blood to be encouraged in his love for her. Her man had not yet been taught all that the corroboree was inaugurated to teach, but that did not prevent her from choosing a cleft between two great weathering sandstone rocks on the top of a ridge to watch for her man's return from the chase. The red figure was the first object to strike the eyes of the returning tribe of hunters. The red cloak was the only object looked for by the young man. But one night Krubi's heart was saddened. She learned that there was to be a great corroboree, and her man was to be taught what—to do in war. Blacks from another tribe had been seen on Burragorang preserves.

They were to be punished.

Krubi of the red cloak stood on the sandstone cleft and watched for the return of the warriors. She heard the yells of battle. She saw here and there a flying figure, and sometimes she saw the swaying crowds down on the clear patches between the forest giants and tangled scrubs. Then in the afternoon she saw her scattered tribe of fighting men returning, and no young, lithe figure stepped out from the others and peered up as of yore.

Krubi stayed for seven days waiting, and her tears formed a little rivulet, and already the Leptospermum and the Boronia serrulata, and Epacris longifolia had begun to sprout. Krubi did not know their names, neither did Camoola, but Camoola showed the flowers-the Buttonflower, the Native Rose, and the Native Fuchsiaand afterwards the botanists made the names.

Then Krubi went to the camp.

The ashes were cold and seven days old.

So Krubi returned to the sandstone ridge, and, with that power that the black man exercises, and that all mankind possesses, she willed herself to die. She passed into the little tract of weathered

9

sandstone, and up came the most beautiful of Australian flora. The stalk is firm and straight, and without a blemish, just like the man Krubi died for. The leaves are serrated and have points just like his spear. And the flower is red, redder and more glowing than any other in Australia. The black man called it "waratah" because it is most beautiful. He loved it because he knew its history.

And Sir James Smith, the President of the Royal Society in London, wrote of it in his book published in 1793 in these words: "The most magnificent flower that the prolific soil of New Holland affords is, by common consent, both of Europeans and natives, the WARATAH!"

No one but an Australian can say, "My Waratah," for no other country has it.

Mr. Richard T. Baker, F.L.S., of Sydney, has produced a book called "The Australian Flora in Applied Art" 1915. Get it and see for yourself what a wonder this flower is!

THE FIRST GYMEA OR GIGANTIC LILY

One of the most wonderful of Australian flowers is the New South Wales variety of Gymea or Gigantic Lily (Doryanthes excelsa). This huge red bloom of ours is, as its variety name implies, the most gorgeous of the Doryanthes genus in this country.

The legend the natives have about it is as follows:-

One still, hot day in a summer of ages and ages ago, a tribe of aborigines found sustenance in a river-bed that lay at the bottom of a wooded ravine. The whole season had been droughty, and the water was hardly running at all. Yet there were holes, and great wide holes too, wherein the water was so deep that no one knew of any tree that would reach down to the bottom. Stones thrown in fell with a heavy, full-sounding splash and were sucked down and down. In those murky depths were huge eels and giant fish, and occasionally one or other came to the surface and fell a victim to the spears of the black men. The great towering, rock-girt side of the river gave many hours' shelter from the burning, blazing sun. That side with the easterly aspect was clothed with many myrtles and much Macrozamia[3] and Chorizema[4] and bracken fern. Quite a number of the dainty, feathery Christmas Bushes (Ceratopetalum gummiferum) shone gorgeous and red amid the myrtaceae, and rearing high above all the undergrowth were the giant eucalypti-the Eucalyptus Smithii with its long, narrow leaf, E. Saligna or Sydney Blue Gum, the Eucalyptus australiana or peppermint, and others-while wild clematis and Wonga wonga[5] vine climbed from shrub to shrub.

That day the heat was intense.

Nothing of the vegetation stirred, excepting during the silent wandering of a truant zephyr that came floating up the river-gully

---

3 Macrozamia-burrawang.
4 Chorizema-a yellow-flowered shrub.
5 Wonga-Teooma australis.

like the long, balanced, weightless gossamer that sways when the web is broken in the early morning.

The tribe lay about under the clematis and creeper and amongst the ferns. Only the hardiest of the hunting men stood, silent and perspiring, with poised spear, waiting for a fish to sail up to the top. Now and then a little chewed burley from the seed of the burrawang was softly dropped to the water.

Otherwise all was still.

Even the dogs lay stretched and asleep. They were too languid when awake to move with the shadows.

The fishing had been good. A number of splendid carp lay in a cool watered crack between the great flat rocks. When one of these fish appeared amongst the burley the thrust of spear was lightning-like. It made hardly a ripple, yet it pierced the water deep. It was so smartly withdrawn that the fish had scarcely time to cause even a bubble. By a dexterous heave it was landed, and it lay to kick its life away in that crack between the rocks.

Suddenly from away in the south-west a great billowing cloud hove into view above the cliff and above the gum-tops. Then the wandering zephyr became fierce. It swept on its way and brought down a shower of rustling leaves.

A haze, deep and sombre, crowded the scene. It was changed.

The fishermen glanced upwards, and then at one another.

They knew.

Up the gully came a boisterous gust. The placid water became a mass of dense ripples in a moment. They dashed their little wavelets in spiteful spray against the rocks. It was useless to fish any more. Besides, an eerie feeling was abroad. The dogs whimpered and huddled near some black or other-man, woman, or child., The old white-haired chief stalked out into the sand patch that lay athwart the dwindled stream, and cast a thoughtful glance at the heavens. The children cowered. The whole camp became astir, and yet no one seemed to know just where to go nor just what to do. Women shivered and drew their 'possum rugs closer over their shoulders, and children's teeth chattered. They were susceptible and apprehensive.

Suddenly, too, the air was darkened, for the huge woolly mass of cloud had encompassed the whole firmament, and blotted out the sun. Gusts roared louder and louder. The myrtles seethed and rustled and quivered and bent before it. Huge tree-tops swayed and shook, and their interlaced branches tore and fought. A solitary bird high above essayed to cross the gully, but was swept from its course and whirled out of sight down stream. Now a great branch twirled and was snapped, and came crashing through the undergrowth and lobbed on the ground with a dull thud.

All the fishermen but one retreated. The one stood still. He was a mighty man and the son of a chief—

Then came the thunder. It pealed amongst the timber and amongst the people. With it came the blinding flash and the driven rain.

The chief led the way. The whole tribe rushed to a cave they knew of. It was formed by the rolling, some long years before, of three huge boulders against one another in such a way that an entrance was left, and inside was room for several hundred people. The last to enter was the chief's son. As he came another terrific crash of thunder and a fearful flash of lightning tore the world. Women put their hands to their eyes and ears, and children screamed. Men were struck dumb with terror. Peal on peal, flash on flash came, and then a deluge poured down outside, whilst the wanton gale swung the timber and felled the great gums. Then came the most awful flash of all.

In a lull in the downpour something happened. Flame and sound came at the same second. The clustering boulders were struck. A gum was splintered and shattered, and the whole earth, it seemed to the frightened tribe, was smitten, and it groaned and was hurled into space. The great masses of rock shifted, and the entrance was closed. Utter darkness fell in there. It was a thing that had never happened to their world before.

The chief's son now felt that he had to do something to prove that he was fit to rule when his old father passed away. The white-haired, wrinkled man was too spent with his years to do anything. Somewhere in the dark amongst his people he sat, and spoke not a word.

But the young man moved. He crawled cautiously inwards, his hands always scouting before him. If he touched a wall he turned and tried another direction.

He came to a passage so narrow and jagged that he cut his knees and his forehead. But he kept on. Once he had to pull away a stone or two in order to go further. At last he espied a thin streak of daylight. It came down from the top. It was very wispy, but up there somewhere was the light of day.

He listened.

There was no sound of thunder and no feel of rain. The giant storm had passed on down the gully more rapidly than it came.

13

Outside a faint rumbling might then have been heard, but it was already far away. The appalling bursts of wind had passed on, too, and all was still again. Out of a clear, clean, blue sky the sun poured its westering beams across, and thick columns of swaying mists rose up into that space from which, as rain, they had come. Nature was smiling now, and the world was better for the storm. A mass of broken green and leafy twigs lay on the ground or were caught in the vines, and many floated, water-logged, on the pools. But down underground a whole tribe lay imprisoned and afraid to move.

All but the chief's son. He was now sensing the beauties of a clarified day outside because of the tiny streak of light that was with him.

A little more pushing and he came to the bottom of a shaft. He could move a little dêbris and wrack, and he found that in the shaft he could stand upright. He could see the blue sky above. He stooped and coo-eed.

He was answered.

Then he lost his head, and he flung up his arms and commenced to climb. Like a rock wallaby he squeezed himself up and up. Pressing first one side and then the other, he forced his way towards the top. He loosened stones and rubbish, and they fell to the bottom. But he kept going on up. Near the entrance one boulder was poised. He placed his weight upon it and it was loosened. It crashed to the bottom, and that stopped any other person from following the chief's son. He nearly went down with it. A handy branch was his salvation. He grasped it, and with a mighty heave he was out of the pit.

He was saved.

And what of the rest? He leaned over and shouted. He heard the answer faint below. But the loosened sides were still falling. He tried all around and about, but there was no chance of getting between those enormous rocks. The marks of the lightning were upon them. A wonderful pattern of a tree was indelibly burnt into the stone, and is there till this day.

We have heard it said that the place is in George's River, somewhere behind Glenfield or Minto.

The sun sank as he does at the close of every day, and night fell quickly down in the river. Up on the boulders the chief's son slumbered.

Down below his people cried themselves to sleep. In the morning hunger took possession. Everyone must eat. The great fish still lay down near the water-holes. The escaped man sped there. He gathered up the fish, as many as he could carry, and took them up to the mouth of the shaft. Then he got some sarsaparilla vine, and with it and some rush he made a rope. Then he raced back, and began to climb the rock again.

He slipped.

Oh, agony! He was falling down, down. Crash! He rolled, and in rolling a jagged limb tore him badly.

He was pierced and his abdomen was cut badly.

But his thought for his people conquered the pain.

He got up again.

For days he fed them thus.

He grew weaker and weaker, but he fished and he fed the people. None could get out to him. He could simply lower as much food as possible. Some would live while others would die. This continued for many days. Those who told the tale to white men said that it lasted for a whole year.

Yet down in the prison the people were dying.

Then the tribe from Kurnell penetrated to behind Glenfield or Minto. They had found no opposition and no sign of the George's River blacks in any of their excursions for this whole year, so they became more and more emboldened, and the fishing and hunting were good. By the time they reached the place of the tragedy the chief's son was very ill indeed. His wound had never healed. He kept it open by his climbing up and his getting down. And the day came when the Kurnell blacks were very near.

He heard them.

He lay down under the shade of some Christmas Bush and Waratahs. The blooms were out and they shone red. He loved the waratah. He knew its story, and he had many times sucked the sweet nectar from its flowers. Beside him grew a little plant. He knew no use for it. But it was destined to be of great use to him.

Now up the stream he knew of a trickling spring. Another gully wound down its twisted way from above and opened into the bed of the river. It was very narrow, and in wet weather a little torrent splashed down from the flatter country above, and by means of a leaping waterfall it joined the more swollen river. Its sides were far more dense than the steep sides of the river. The Leptospermum flourished there, and waratahs were in crimson splendour. Out from a rock wall at the side gushed the spring. In dry times It simply was swallowed up in peaty ground beneath the tea-tree and Leptospermum and Ceratopetalums, but in rainy times it o'erbore them and joined the river.

A spirit often came out from that glen. It was speckled with glowing fires that flashed and were covered, and flashed and were covered, over and over again. The spirit was light and ethereal, for it could never be seen in its entirety and it could never be heard. All the tribe knew of it, and all held it in awe. All but the medicine man, and he, sometimes, when he had donned the mystic pipe-clay bands, went right up to the spring and talked with it there. When he came back he bore with him beautiful bunches of ferns of many kinds-Hymenophyllum and Asplenium, portions of the fronds of the Dicksonia, the Adiantum, the Alsophila, excelsa, the Umbrella fern, the Acrostichurn and others.

It must have been the spirit that came to the hero of this legend, for as he lay exhausted someone took his hand and placed it on the little amaryllis that seemed to him to be of no use. Immediately it moved and grew. The leaves stretched up and up and became broader and broader. It was a wonderful happening. Many leaves came, each one long and broad and supple, and out from the central part came a long firm stalk. It grew up and up until at several feet a flower formed.

The young man's wound was more painful now than ever before. He pressed his hand to it and he found it to be bleeding. Then he swung his hand over to that wonderful plant again and it became red with his blood.

And it was warm.

It is always warm.

The young black slept. How long he slept no one knows. Whether it was for hours, or days, or years, has never been told, but when he awoke he was being well cared for. About his body was drawn one of the leaves of the doryanthes excelsa. Out from his mia-mia he saw many of these plants. They had come while he slept. All had leaves like bandages, and many had stalks with great red buds to crown them. They would be burst soon, and a flower as red as the waratah would be there.

Women came and peeped at him. Children saw that he was awake, and they laughed for joy.

Then a woman bent over him and deftly she wove another leaf bandage around him. The old fern-root poultices, dried up, lay around about. Then he knew who had tended him when he slept. And he felt strong enough to get up.

Close by were the fallen rocks. There was still no way in or out.

So the first Gymea or Gigantic Lily came into being, and not long ago men dug under the boulders and found a great heap of aboriginal bones.

WHY THE TURTLE HAS NO TAIL

The Australian aborigines believed that the Milky Way was a "pukkan" or track, along which many spirits of departed blacks travelled to heaven, and that the dark place that we call Magellan's Cloud was a hole or split that occurred when the universe was frightfully shaken by some mighty upheaval which gave us many of the wonders of Nature, including the brilliant waratah, gorgeous caves such as Jenolan and others less magnificent, burnt patches of rock, and so on.

Legends also make mention of a hidden river, over which certain spirits have to travel to a Promised Land. This river flowed at the edge of a mighty forest, and beyond a fearful range of huge jagged mountains, at the nearer foot of which lay an extensive marshy lake, in the centre of which was an enchanted island. The natives of the South-East of Australia were very clear about the picture just described. They said that not only had some people spoken to returned men who had waded through the lake and been on the island and climbed the mountain and nearly reached the river, but they had also had amongst them at one time and another living men who had seen these fairy places and always knew that a continuous stream of spirits passed that way to the Unseen River.

Two giant trees grew on the bank, and a tortoise lay athwart it. Up to the time of this happening all tortoises and turtles had long tails. This tortoise reached from the bank just opposite the big trees, to the other.

On the journey many spirits were supposed to be in some way tempted to do evil, and succumbed to the temptation; therefore there were some fallings by the way. Some were kept floundering about in the lake itself, and these congregated on the island until they had expiated their sins, when they were allowed to go on. Others failed when climbing the mountain, and there on some barren peak they had to wait, while others remained faithful until reaching the lower level, and then were within sight of the river. But there was a test for them. They had to squeeze between the trunks of the giant trees, and then the bridge they reached was the tortoise.

Then came a time when many people quite good enough to get into heaven failed to reach the opposite bank of the river. It was known that they had got between the trees, and then all trace of them was lost; but one day a man arrived amongst the people who had been remade, and he told them his experiences.

He said that he had died and reached the tortoise on the unseen river. He stepped upon it, and was half way along it when it gave a sly jerk, and he fell off its tail into the river. He was borne along very swiftly, for it is a fast flowing stream, and suddenly he was swept underground. For a long time he was carried through deep subterranean passages, and at last he came out into sunlight. He found himself still in a river, and now it flowed between high banks, and playing in it were blacks that he knew. Some were just swimming, some were fishing, some were hiding in the rushes awaiting ducks. They did not know of his presence, though some seemed to hear him, for they suddenly became afraid and rushed off to their camp. At last he was swept into the sea, and a great wave washed him ashore. As soon as he touched land he found that he was changing. It took a long time, but at last he became a man again, and when he looked at his chest and felt his back he was aware of the scars that he 'had borne in his other existence.

He now suggested that when the next great man died—the chief or the doctor or the rainmaker or the clergyman—his best stone axe be buried with him.

Then a sorcerer came forward and proclaimed that he would undertake to go to the river and secure the passage of it for all time. He selected some other brave people, and by the aid of his sorcery he set out on the way of the spirits. He soon reached the forest, but found it full of the "little men of the bush." They barred the way of the party. Try as they would, no passage through the ranks of the "little men" could be made. So then they turned and followed the flow of the river, and that way no opposition was offered.

They came to a tree even higher than those at the crossing-place, and up that the great sorcerer climbed. From the top of it he could see the spirits stepping on to tail of the tortoise and some being shaken off. Many of these were taken by the claws of the hind feet of the beast and afterwards eaten. Others were carried down stream. The shadow of the tree was impenetrable to the "little men," and a bright star shed a beam to the tortoise.

The sorcerer saw that he must die before he could pass the little men and he and his party returned home. He sharpened again his axe. He put a sharpened bone in the fire, and scraped some of the burnt part off into his food. Then he died, and as a good spirit, he reached the giant trees, and there were no "little men" to stop him. But in their place was a great snake that reared its head and prepared to strike.

With a blow of his axe he severed the head from the body, and picking it up he squeezed between the trees and stepped on to the tail of the tortoise. When he was about half way over, just as he had seen it do to others, and just as the returned man had told it did to him, it gave a great shake. But he was wary, and with another great blow of his axe he cut the tail off. Quickly rushing to the other bank he turned and swung the axe at the head of the tortoise and that was severed too. Of this, though, he repented, and as the head swung down the stream he put the head of the snake in its place. Then the beast rolled over and sank out of sight.

And so now all tortoises and turtles have a snake's head and are tail-less.

And if the last woman of the Illawarra Group, who is still living, is asked about it, and if all the points of the story are examined, it will be found that there is as much truth as fiction in it.

Those who ask, however, must have the right sympathy or they will hear nothing.

THE FLOOD

The natives of the head waters of the Murray River, or as it is more correctly called, the Hume River, had a story of a Deluge. Whether this is identical with our Biblical story of the Flood, when Sisit, or Noah, was advised to build an Ark and take animals into it for the preservation of himself by providing his meat foods, and with the New Zealand Maori's account of a Flood that covered the whole world, is not clear. Our aborigines had no idea of so extensive a submersion of the Earth as that.

But they did say that water covered a very great extent of country, and all were drowned but two people. It was timed to be in what the Central Australian natives call vaguely "the Alcheringa," and by that they meant that they did not know when nor where, but from it was born a separate race of human kind. The word "Alcheringa" was never used except when at the time and from the happening an ancestor was brought into being.

The worship of the blacks was always ancestor worship. They believed in many gods, and one God would and did make other gods. They had no conception of one God only. All. gods were equal, and came at the "Alcheringa" period or era. Since that era there have been no gods born, they said, and they did not expect any. There was, in their belief, no "Second Coming."

There was to be a betrothal.

A boy of a certain family group was, when he grew up, to be the husband of a woman of another family group belonging to another tribe or race.

But no one could fix upon any girl. All the girl babies that were born were closely examined by the old priest of the boy's family group, but none could he see of which he could say that it was the one he was looking for. Meanwhile the boy was growing up, and the time drew near when he was to be taught in the proper school or corroboree what it was right for him to know. And he was proving to be a very fine type of boy. He outshone all the others in looks and build and feats of boy-strength.

Now it happened that there was one article of food that he was not permitted to eat. That was the fruit of the Styphelia triflora-a sort of five-corner. The Astroloma pinifolium, which is something like the Styphelia, he could eat, and he was very fond of it. He gathered it in plenty, and he pounded it and mixed the flour of it with water from the river, and when he had made a cake of it he roasted it upon the embers of the fires that were left by his mother.

In his searching for his favourite fruit he travelled far, for he came over the range to the coast, and there he fell in with another tribe. With them he travelled north, and must have penetrated into the district of Illawarra, which is the most beautiful part of Australia, and has been called the "Garden of New South Wales." The pity is that another part has filched for land-booming purposes, the beautiful aboriginal name of "Illawarra," and applied it to a part that has no claim to be called a garden, and the people of Illawarra have allowed it, and have become content to call their district "The South Coast," which it in turn has no claim to.

Here he found the Achras australe or Brush Apple. This was not his totem, but he did not know that, and with the rest of the people he ate it. Immediately he was seized with a longing to taste the Styphelia triflora's fruit and he set out to find the way back to his own people. He crossed the Shoalhaven River and journeyed night and day down the coast. All the people whom he met were very friendly and would have made him welcome with them, but he did not stay. They saw his fine proportions and superior bearing, and in their ignorance and superstition they soon accounted for his appearance by crediting him with supernatural powers.

He passed right on under the Pigeon House which was, years and years afterwards, noticed by Captain Cook, and over what we know as the Clyde River, and then he headed up amongst the huge mountains and tremendous gorges, on and on, until he espied the familiar peaks of his own country. He could then look away to the west. In the distance on his left hand he saw the bold, snow-covered peaks and crags of our Mount Kosciusko, which is the highest peak in Australia. This youth of the time of the Alcheringa had grown, during his travels, into a young man, and yet he had had no chance to be initiated into the secrets and mysteries of his station.

While journeying on the great heights of the mountains he chanced upon a certain cave. There were no people near that he could see, and yet in it he found a bundle of spears and boomerangs, and other implements. He chose one of the best of the spears and stood gazing upon it, for it was of very fine workmanship. The head was of a material he had never seen before. It was white and

21

shining, and its point and barbs were very sharp and extremely hard. He believed it to be made of a stone that did not exist anywhere in the country that he knew of. In this he was right for its presence there was the result of a wonderful system of barter that was practised in those days. Natives of the coast, especially those whose ancestor was responsible for the existence of the Livistona Palms, traded the heart of the palm for the hard quartzite of the far-distant districts. They sent the white, nutty heart of the palm through the various family groups and tribes until it reached those who had the coveted spearheads, and by the same manner of conveyance the spearheads reached the man who obtained the other article. Sometimes it took many months for the exchange to be completed, but in no instance was any unfair dealing resorted to.

Suddenly the young aborigine dropped the spear back on the bundle. It was not his. Though he had never been to school he knew that it was wrong to take it. He left the cave, and rounding a cliff he saw another. In it were sticks of a different pattern. But they were, all but one, wrapped up in bark and tied round with rushes. The one was lying uncovered and enclosed in the bones of a human hand. The skeleton lay near. Someone had been handling the stick, and in handling it died. The youth was afraid. He turned about in the cave and looked out. His quick eyes were keen in their glance, and there down below him he saw a native peering from behind a eucalyptus tree.

This native chanced to be the rainmaker of his particular tribe. He had been preparing the ground for the rainmaking ceremony. He had seen the youth. No action of his was missed. And the rainmaker was pleased. He made friendly signs and then he came to the cave. In one side of it was a deposit of red ochre. The rainmaker got some of that, and taking a short piece of waratah stick from his hair in which it was concealed he smeared it with red ochre. Then he "sang" it.

This was a strange sight to the youth. He knew nothing of ceremony. He gazed in wonder at the rainmaker, who saw that he was uninitiated.

Then the rainmaker did wrong. He was so overjoyed to find so fine and comely a youth quite ignorant of the arts and magic of great people that his vanity became overpowering, and he danced and sang in his delight. As he danced he gave way to such an exultation that he jumped amongst the bones of the skeleton and he disturbed the piece of wood and turned it over. Then he saw that it had strange markings and many hieroglyphics. He bent down and seized it and swung it in the air and tossed it from hand to hand.

22

He kept this up until he was exhausted, and then he sat down and examined what he had picked up. There were marks on it that he understood. It was the sacred stick of the rainmaker of thousands of years before. So he "sang" that too.

To "sing" anything was to utter incantations or prayers while looking at it, and that praying was supposed to give the article or the ancestor who caused it to come into being the power to bring about a certain wished-for result. Of course there was much more to be done than just to pray. There were mostly many ceremonies to be gone through, and as many as twelve months were required in which to complete some, what may be termed, services.

He poised the stick upon his open palm, and marching round the cave like Germans doing the goose-step, he balanced it first on the middle of his palm, and then worked it along to the tip of his index finger, then back and up his forearm, and again to his palm. All the time he was doing this he was uttering a chant. It was a prayer to the ancestor of his family group, who fell from heaven in a rain and entered the side of a mountain not far away.

Then he asked the youth to accompany him to the site that he had marked out as the church where he was to begin the ceremony that would cause rain.

From this point smoke could be seen curling its wisps up through the eucalyptus trees where the remainder of the group-people awaited the call of the rainmaker.

Putting his hands to his mouth he coo-eed.

This was answered from below.

Then he called and told his people to come up, intimating that if all did not come he would make rain that would never stop and all the creeks would become swollen, tearing, smashing, crashing torrents of destruction, and all the rocks would tumble down and the great mountains would be washed level: and Mount Kosciusko would shed its mantle of snow and everybody would be killed or drowned but him. He would cause the sacred stick to grow into a great tree that would reach up to heaven, and he only would be able to climb it and thus reach where the flood did not come.

Then he told them that he would not like to cause the death of the stranger that was with him. But he would make the stranger as his son.

Then someone asked what stranger he meant.

So he told the youth to go down to the people and show himself.

On the way there were some Styphelias. The youth plucked the berries and crushed them and ate them. From that moment his eyes were opened. He saw evil as well as good. The evil seemed best.

23

Now amongst the people there was a maiden who brushed close to the youth as he walked. And she, too, was eating styphelias. The youth offered her some of what he had, and they stopped to eat together. The rest went on up to the church, and already the rainmaker had begun the service.

He had marked himself with the red ochre and he held the sacred stick that he got in the cave. He had no idea but that the youth he had met was somewhere with the people and was seeing for the first time the sacred service or ceremony or corroboree or whatever we like to call it. So he put far more vim into it than he otherwise would have done. He told of the sacred stick that he had, and the more he talked the more excited he grew. He even went so far as to say that the strange youth was brought by him into the cave and that henceforth he would be of great service in assisting to bring rain.

Then he asked that the youth come forward.

There was no answer.

He called in a loud voice and the people looked all around. The women and children who were sitting some distance back from the men also looked all about. There was no sign of the strange youth and no sign either of one of the maidens of the tribe.

They told the rainmaker.

He became very angry. He made one more appeal to the rain ancestor to send rain down and then he brought the proceedings to a close. He erased all the marks that he had drawn on the ground. He rubbed all the drawings from his body. At last he threw the sacred stick with such force to the ground that it was smashed to pieces, and he ordered the men to scatter through the forest and into the gullies and about the rocky hillsides until the youth and maiden were found.

He asked the advice, however, of the chief, and the old warrior gave him permission to order as he would. He must, however, not go himself, for the chief was afraid of his magic and he wanted to stay beside him until the rain came.

Then from out the place where the broken sacred stick was flung a river gushed. It poured down amongst the women and children. The strong sun drew much of it up into the sky and clouds were quickly formed. They turned to rain, and so water was pouring out from the earth and out from the sky. Big trees were being washed out by the roots, and great rocks began to fall and to hurtle down the slopes. The whole mountain soon became a crashing mass of trees and shifting boulders and earth slides, and the valleys were being filled with water and débris. All the sacred sticks were washed out of the cave and were whirled about in the water with the trees and all the other wrack.

This went on until not a mountain top could be seen, and every tree was either covered with water or was felled.

Every tree save one.

One tree showed up above the whole flood.

And in its branches were four people.

The rainmaker was one. The strange youth and the girl who ate styphelia berries with him were there, and so, too, was the old priest of the boy's own tribe who had been searching for the girl to be betrothed to him.

This old man was the only person on earth now who could say whether or not the youth and the girl were to be man and wife. Up there on the tree-tops he bade them to do nothing that would bring upon them the wrath of the magic that lay all around and about the world.

But what troubled them most was how to send the waters all away so that they could come down and eat and live. Somehow it was known that the boy had eaten of the forbidden styphelia fruit and he had to be purged of it.

So they tried all ways that they could think of to make him sick, and at last they succeeded. He became so weak under the treatment that he would have fallen into the water and been drowned had not the girl wrapped her long hair about him and tied both him and herself to the bough.

The rainmaker, too, fell ill. He had done great wrong and he was mostly responsible for the calamity that had overtaken the world. While the boy was recovering the rainmaker was becoming worse. The priest and the youth talked about it and it was agreed that the rainmaker must die. Not until he passed away would the flood go down argued the priest, and when he became quite convinced about it, he simply pushed the sick sinner into the water, and he sank and was no more.

During the night the flood went down and the marooned persons descended to the earth.

The only eatable thing was the berry of the styphelia. Not one of that plant was destroyed. Even those that grew amongst the fallen mountains were not killed but survived in the wet mud that was everywhere.

And that, the youth dare not eat.

Now growing deep down in a crevice between some fallen boulders was a plant called "Native Flax."

25

It has a seed that is wrapped round with a furry material, and no one would think that it is good for food.

But the youth was very hungry and he thought he would try it.

It was quite sweet and full of oil. So that kept him alive while the others ate styphelia.

Birds soon came back from somewhere and because they still were wet, for the sun was not strong after the great flood, they were easily caught.

And the Owenia acidula or "mooley plums" quickly grew and ripened.

And the waratahs bloomed, each flower giving many drops of sweet honeyed juice.

One day the girl was not to be found. Both the old priest and the young man searched everywhere for her, and they could find only very few traces. There were some, and these they followed until it became too dark to go further. The priest lit a fire, and there, before its faint light, in the dense bush, with towering new-formed mountains and heaps of the earth shutting them in, the young aborigine was inducted into the usages and the beliefs of his people concerning marrying and giving in marriage.

There were many things that a woman must never be allowed to do. She would undertake the things that even she herself did not want and if her husband allowed this, much ill would result. There was, too, certain work that was hers and hers alone. The only food that she had to provide was the yam that could be dug out of the ground. She must always carry a short, pointed yamstick. If a family bereavement occurred she had to show her sorrow only in certain ways, and it was the province of her husband to see to it that she did it. Men had to show sorrow in other ways and for other occurrences.

All that sort of thing was told to the young man, and the telling of it was accompanied with much handshaking and body patting and it lasted far into the night.

All the necessary vows were taken, and a record of it was made by the priest on his sacred stick. He had cut the stick from a callitris, or Cyprus pine, and already he had inscribed a good many stories.

Next day the girl came back.

She had never been far away, and she was watching for just what she saw.

So from then on they were man and wife, and the old priest went into a cave and died. He took with him his sacred stick, and hundreds of years afterwards-perhaps thousands-Tom Adamson found some remains of him not far from Adaminaby. Tom took the stick to the blacks, and they knew all the story. They said that they

26

were descended from that youth and that maiden, but that, of course, their real ancestor was very far back from them. Tom was just the sort of man to whom the aborigines told the things that they were usually too shy to tell. The old humbugs of priests knew their own duplicity, and in spite of the hold that they had upon the rest, they were always afraid that white men would find them out.

They often thought that the white men were reincarnations of their own holy men. So for that reason was much of their secretiveness. And those who did not pretend to have seen burning bushes that were not consumed, and tables of stone that were miraculously written upon, were afraid of the magic that was hidden everywhere, and could be called into play by the old priestly humbugs.

There is a peculiar hole near the road with the marks of the natives all round it. They said that out of it at long, long periods many living blacks came, and always amongst them was a clever rainmaker. and at least one who belonged to the styphelia totem, and he must not eat of the fruit of the plant. Should he do so he would bring upon the people some great ill-probably cause another rainmaker to so conduct himself as to bring down another flood.

HOW THE WARATAH GOT ITS HONEY

Krubi was the name of the beautiful black girl who became a waratah, and amongst the aborigines of the Burragorang Valley the name is only given to one girl of any tribe, of all its branches; and then only when the mother or the father has been reckoned to be very good looking, and the child is expected, therefore, to bear the same advantage (if advantage it is); so that not a baby girl can be christened Krubi until the former Krubi is dead.

THE STORY

Once upon a time, not long after the original Krubi had become a waratah plant, and her red cloak had made the brilliant hue of the flower, and only a very few other Krubis had ever been so named, a young lubra wife had determined that should she ever have a girl baby it must bear the coveted name. The living Krubi was very old, and already she had more than once failed to carry what her youngest child had put into her dilly-bag. That was the sign that her husband could leave her to the care of that youngest child, instead of staying back to aid her along.

The young wife wished for old Krubi's death very much. She was never far away when Krubi was being assisted by Warrindie, the youngest Of her family. But never did the good-looking lubra (Woolyan) so much as place her hand under Krubi's elbow.

But Krubi was wonderfully tenacious of life. She battled on.

She was relieved from all work. She had only to carry the dilly-bag when the tribe were moving, and they did not move much.

Woolyan grew very anxious. Her longing for the death of Krubi grew a passion. At last she determined to "bone" Krubi. No woman had ever done that. Only the men of her tribe were accustomed to kill by "boning."

So Woolyan picked out the fine shinbone of a big dingo, and she

28

rubbed it with sand from the bed of the creek until it was white and smooth, and she hid it in her hair, awaiting the time when she could catch Krubi alone.

Many days sped by; several moons came and went.

Then the blacks determined to have a corroboree.

A good young man had been having private lessons in the things that were taught which Krubi and Woolyan and the other women were not permitted to see, and then came the great night.

It was very dark. A space had been cleared amongst the giant gum trees. But whilst it was still daylight the young women had chosen their places. Woolyan was delighted to see that Krubi was not well enough to take her place in the little march that the active old women made. So she got up from her place, and going back to Krubi, she hurriedly undid her hair that she had done up to hold the bone concealed, but before she could catch hold of it the thing fell to the ground.

Old Krubi saw it.

Then did old age give place to greater activity than youth possessed. With a bound and a yell Krubi jumped forward and stamped her foot on the death-dealing bone.

And Krubi's youngest bounded too. Woolyan was caught in a grip that she could not shake off, and blow after blow found her face and head and shoulders.

The corroboree was abandoned. The tribe surrounded the fighting women. But the chief demanded that the hubbub stop, and Krubi tell the cause of the trouble.

The sentence upon Woolyan was death. Before she was to die she "went bush." The beautiful waratahs were in bloom, and when Woolyan saw them all her false pride and hatred left her.

Kneeling beside a plant covered with the beautiful red flowers, her tears fell into them. They were tears of repentance. And as she wept her child was born.

She laid it at the foot of a waratah bush.

When the men who were to club her to death came and saw her they were filled with a great compassion.

So they sent for old Krubi.

There was a great reconciliation, and the tears of both women fell into the waratahs.

Woolyan's husband happened to smell the blooms and the scent was good. He plucked one separate flower, and the liquid within it crept into his fingers, He put them into his mouth, and, lo, the taste was very sweet!

So that day the waratah became a further source of comfort to the aborigines.

Sir James Smith wrote of it in 1793: "It is, moreover, a great favourite with the natives upon account of a rich honeyed juice which they sip from its flowers."

WHY THE SUN SETS

Out on the Murrumbidgee there is a tale about the setting sun. The country there is very different from what it is where the aborigines had a story of the Escapees.

It is flat.

It seems to be below, far below, the level of the sea.

And the sun can be seen setting.

The land which contains the great, dreary salt lakes-Frome, Eyre, Gardiner, Amadeus, Torrens, and a lot of others named and unnamed, is really below the sea's level, and if ever a canal is cut from the head of Spencer Gulf to the bed of those lakes a vast extent of territory will become an ultra-salt inland sea.

But though the country through which the greater part of the Murrumbidgee and the Lachlan and the Darling flow seems very low, it is still above the level of the great oceans.

It seems to be a disc, like a huge plate.

Turn which way one will, the horizon is sharp and level and lies all around. In the summer (and summer sets in in October and lasts until the end of March) the sun rises a huge fiery red ball. Before he appears he sends his torrid shafts, and the earth is dried and heated. With his horrible advance agents of wilting beams the flies are a wracking buzz and a stinging poison as they wing their nauseous way about, and all the other insect life starts into pestering being.

The smell of baked earth rises, and the dried grasses stand stiffly and starkly.

The level east lightens; and slowly, surely, and relentlessly the great red disc ascends and throws long shadows across the ground.

The dwarfed and gnarled gums seem to beg for some respite. The sombre Murray Pines cluster in masses as if seeking the solace and protection of one another's company.

By the advent of the first month of summer the few orchids that bloomed in the short spring have gone, and the glowing grasses have seeded and died.

It is now a bare and browned and sere world.

The sun changes from red to grey, and as he wends his solemn way up to the zenith he pours out molten light.

Lazy clouds of dust rise up from the new-formed roads, stirred by waggoned teams, and flatten and float out over the trees.

Shadows grow less and less until they are only patches directly below the bushes.

Life is a dreary and painful process.

Horses stand mutely, head to tail, close to any tree stumps that may be there; sheep huddle, panting, out in the glaring sun; birds sit on the boughs with wings opened and mouths agape; nothing lives in the wilting day-everything crouches in whatever of shade can be found.

Over and above passes the molten ball, and as he slowly descends towards the horizon of the west, and the east begins to blacken, life stirs again, and all beings long for the cool of night.

Many nights are but little cooler than the day.

The gay, glowing flowers of the sandstone elevations are not here. No epacrids, no boronias, no waratahs!

The deep restful greens of the laurels, and the glowing browns of the turpentines and woollybutts and ironbarks and lilly-pillies do not show. The banksias are stunted. Only the hardiest trees grow, and the most transient of the grasses, and they are poor and bare-all except the annual grasses. They are the saving of the land.

It was not always so.

The aborigines have a legend-born of their stricken condition, and of that wonderful and unexplainable knowledge of their past history as is revealed to us by our geologists and scientists-which tells of a time when the earth was not parched by such a sun; when it was ever day, but the daylight was the radiance of a human ancestor, and when the trees and shrubs and flowers were as bright and plentiful as they are now in the regions that are not wilted by our sun.

The sun, they say, is an ancestor-a human that was not understood, and he retired in sorrow and became a god and thus came light-so came the setting sun.

A family which claimed the sleeping lizard as its totem was camped in a scrub of Murray Pine (a callitris); and, with wurleys built against a number of seared logs, lived, not far away, a family of which the brown-banded snake was the totem.

During the winter months good rains had fallen, and the ground was clothed with many beautiful grasses and much wild parsley, and rearing its pretty pink three-leaved and fringed flowers amongst the grasses was the Thysanotus tuberosus, or Fringed Violet.

32

The Kennedya and the Hardenbergia clambered over the old time-worn stumps, and the acacias poisoned the air with their pollen.

Down on the ground were the purple and white wild violets. The sleeping lizards fraternised good-naturedly with the snake-people, and all "was merry as a marriage bell."

There was a plethora of foods-birds, animals, roots, and berries.

Amongst the snake people two young men strove for the one maiden, and there had been many quarrels because no one seemed to know to which she had been promised.

Meeting after meeting had been called, and the clamour at every one was great.

At last it was decided that he who made the finest stone spear-head for presentation to the father of the girl should have her.

She often spent many hours running from one to the other and she was not innocent of jeering and jibing at both the anxious workmen.

When the proofs of their handicraft were brought to the wurley of the father he pretended to fly into a great rage. He denounced the young men and scoffed at the spearheads-all of them. He rushed to the King and implored him to condemn the lot. He spat on them and flung them amongst the women, who picked them up and flew into as big a pretence of anger as the man.

The contest was renewed and it continued until the pleasant weather had gone, and the light that came from whatever member of the priesthood held the power to so propitiate the light-giver as to vouchsafe day to the world, began to wane, and it was nearly time for another magician to be appointed to carry on.

To the surprise of everyone, one of the contestants proclaimed himself to be the proper magician.

Now the duties pertaining to such an office were many and arduous.

The priest had to spend long periods in prayer and meditation out on the plain by himself. He had to submit to much indignity-even flagellation, and he had to ostracise himself in other ways.

There were not many natives who cared to be considered the special emissary to the ancestor of the light.

And in this young man's case it meant giving up the girl.

But the dispute was not to be settled.

Withdrawing from the contest did not give the other man the right to his claim.

If winning in the set competition could not happen, then some other way must be chosen by the priest.

And he was not in any hurry to give a pronouncement.

In the meantime the girl did not cease her teasing.

She still jeered at both the newly-announced magician and the other contestant.

This became distasteful to the old women, whose charge she was, and they set her to perform many tasks that otherwise would not have fallen to her lot.

Perhaps never before did so young a girl have to grind the grass seeds. She had to find out for herself how to hold the stone between the calves of her legs and how to use the grinder.

She became a wife without being married, for it was a wife's duty to make most of the cakes.

One day she found her suitor to be busy making a shield.

He was drawing the circles and the radiating lines that represented the light of day.

But in it he drew the sleeping lizard.

It was meant as sarcasm, and it was hoped that this piece of portrayed scorn would bring some evil to his rival. He would much have preferred to go on with the competition until one or the other had won. He was becoming anxious to secure the wife, and this delay was beginning to annoy him.

The newly recognised magician was out somewhere in communion with the saints or the spirits or whatever it is that such people have found when they come back with tales of supernatural visitations while they are either figuratively or really eating locusts and wild honey.

Now the artistry of the young man was good.

The girl was really interested.

She sat beside him watching intently every mark.

And as they sat thus the old lightmaker died, and the new one emerged from his solitude and commenced the ceremony of light making so that it would continue.

As he was so young the light nearly went out. The semi-darkness that ensued was bewildering and it struck terror into everyone.

The tribe implored the young magician to put forth every endeavour, and his answer was that without the girl he could not make more light than there was then.

The people looked all around, but they could not see the wanted girl. No one knew where she had gone.

Then they saw that the young lover was missing also.

The light maker grew very angry.

All the gesticulations, all the genuflexions, all the grotesque dancing that were resorted to in anger, he indulged in.

34

His anger grew very real and it communicated itself to his people. Even the King himself became as the rest.

That feeling gave way to despair. Women sat in groups and beat themselves and one another and inflicted severe wounds. Priests hurriedly drew sacred totemic marks on the ground and drew similar designs on the bodies of those whose right it was to bear them. Mitres were fashioned and put on the heads of the higher clergy. Fires were lit to augment the lessened light of the day.

After a while a hunting party was organised to hunt up the missing people, and upon being blessed they seized their spears and shields and bounded off.

The light maker forgot his mission. He yearned for the girl, and without saying a word he betook himself off to search.

After a very long time he found her.

She was living in a slight depression—a crabhole—that is pointed out to-day by all who know this story.

The man with whom she was living was away at the time, and the light maker appealed to her to come to him.

So together they ran, and all the light of day went with them. The further they went the less the light grew until they were right on the edge of the world.

There a son was born to them, and because of the wrong, the father and mother died.

Never since the beginning of the trouble had the daylight been so clear or so strong as before it, and now it was leaving the earth for ever. No one else could ever receive the instructions that would make him a light maker. The great ancestor needed a mediator between himself and the world, and it had to be a lizard man, and now no lizard man knew what to do.

The daylight faded right away.

In its going it was much more beautiful than ever before. Long streaks of gold spread over the sky, and as that faded everything became awestricken, and the world was hushed.

Even now there is that period "while the air 'twixt dark and daylight's standing still."

But the baby that was born away over there grew and became at once a light man. He held direct communion with the great ancestor and he gathered great quantities of light in his hands.

So he set out to find his way back to where he knew his people dwelt. There was one thing he did not do.

He was born with his back to his people, and he did not turn round. He just walked on and on.

He had great waters to travel over, and great beds of sand to travel through, and great forests to find his way in, and great mires to wade across, but he kept going.

He was determined to find his people and to bring them light. So a time came when the tribe saw light breaking away over in the east. It had disappeared on the one hand and it reappeared on the other.

They were overjoyed.

But the priests counselled great caution.

No one knew what to say or do.

The priests and the King said that if they made the wrong ceremony they would lose the light.

So they waited mutely and watched it. There was no welcoming shout. The birds sang to it. The trees nodded to it. Flowers bowed to it. Dewdrops left the earth and flew to it. But men and women were mute because they were afraid that they may do the wrong thing and it would leave them for ever and all their days would be dark and they could not live.

Therefore the light maker sailed over their heads. He went on to the edge of the world where he was born.

The priests said that when they had found out how to worship him he would come down out of the sky and remain with them for ever, but while in ignorance in that respect he would continue to go over their heads and disappear.

They are still in ignorance. That is why there is no sun worship.

The new sun man became more beloved than any had been before, and so the ancestor made him a god like himself, even if the father and mother did do wrong.

And the ancestor sometimes gives him huge quantities of light, and as it is thrown down to the earth it burns and sears and scorches.

So we have summer. If we could only find out how to carry out the proper ceremony of sun worship then there would be no more great heat waves.

This is the tale of the aborigines who live in those parts where the summer is scorching. It accounts for more things than will be seen at first reading.

When the light is not being thrown in large quantities the days are not scorching and the grass is green and the trees are not so dry and the great cracks in the ground are closed up and the little flowers are blooming and all is gay.

WHAT THE MOON IS

There are very many legends concerning the moon, and the writer has succeeded in collecting fully a dozen of them. There is, strangely, much similarity about them all, though some are from parts as far distant from this one, which belongs to the Murray, as Central Queensland.

This is perhaps the prettiest, and was obtained from a young native who lived mostly in a compound at Wahgunyah. He was camped with two gins on a reserve near Burryjaa Station, in N.S.W., and it was with considerable surprise that the writer found him so ready to talk.

Like all aborigines who tell things so close to the supernatural, he continually looked around about in order to be sure he was not overheard either by any other blacks or by spirits. He was afraid that he might inadvertently say something that people of his totem were forbidden to reveal. That night the moon had not yet risen, and it was plain to me that the three were not a little frightened. The lubras stayed in the little gunyah that the man had built, and plainly did not want to be caught eavesdropping.

All the same, they could not forbear to come out to glance towards the hotel. They were fond of whisky.

Here is the story: In the years before history—the Alcheringa-before the river Murray was made, and only a depression existed, a Bunyip visited the place. He came just at nightfall, and he sat on the bank opposite the camp. He was the colour of the gum-tree that afforded him shelter and something to lean against. Behind him was a swamp, and the man who first saw him had been quietly waiting amongst the rushes, kneeling with just his head above the water and with rushes tied about him. He had succeeded in grabbing a few unsuspecting ducks that sailed within reach, and now he was coming, still with rushes tied about him, and with ducks in his hand, back to the camp.

The Bunyip saw him and pressed himself closer against the tree trunk, working himself around it as it was being passed by the hunter. But the hunter detected the movement, and he yelled in his fear. The Bunyip reached out for him, but only succeeded in tearing some of the rushes from him. He scrambled down into the depression and up the bank on the other side, and by that time the people who had heard his yell were alert and watching for him to appear. Amongst the most active and anxious was the young woman to whom he was soon to be married. Indeed, she ran forward to meet him, and she took the ducks from him to relieve him of that slight burden, and she spoke some soothing words to him. Also she laughed at his fear, and when he had rapidly explained what he had seen she laughed the louder.

This caused a fatal delay. The Bunyip heaved himself up the bank, and, seizing the girl, he raced away with her to the swamp.

Without lengthening the story as the aborigine did by describing the consternation of the camp, and the agony of the young man, we will confine ourselves to the doings of the girl. Her struggles in the swamp could be heard even as far off as the camp, but no one could rescue her, for no human being could withstand a Bunyip, especially at night. However, when day dawned, the young man gathered up his spears, and went over to the swamp. He searched for the track of the Bunyip and he found it. Then he caught a number of frogs and tied their legs together and fastened them to a stake that he drove into the ground on the track. All day he waited, and neither saw nor heard anything of the girl nor the Bunyip.

Next day he went there again, and the frogs were gone.

The Bunyip, he thought, had eaten them. So he got some more and tied them and fastened the rush cord to the stake.

Day after day he did this.

His people tried to persuade him to accompany them, for they were about to move their camp, but he steadfastly refused to go. He said that one day the Bunyip would come out for his feed of frogs, and he would slip past into the lair, and his young girl would again be with him, and he would then bring her home.

So they went without him.

Then the day dawned when he saw them. There was misty rain falling, and in it the Bunyip appeared leading the girl. He was coming for his meal, and because of the rain he thought it was night. The man was dreadfully afraid, but he stood his ground. When the Bunyip saw him he roared. When the girl saw him she held out her hands and she wept. The man simply stared into the beast's eyes, and gradually it felt fear. He suddenly threw something at it, but the Bunyip was too quick. He threw a frog and it hit the man in the eye and blinded it. Nothing daunted the man hurled a spear and he blinded one of the Bunyip's eyes. Smarting with pain, the fearsome beast fled, and the man flung himself forward to clasp the girl. But she was under a spell. She was obliged to follow her captor. So a chase commenced. The Bunyip tore through the swamp, over the sandy patch where the prickly hakeas grew and the leptospermums and the banksias were in flower, and pretty blooms like the Actinotus and Thysonotus and Dillwynia and Tetratheca were glowing gaily. He reached the country where eucalypti and callitris, stood, and ran past the sleeping country and a mountain which we call Mount Goombargona. It is a round hill that stands up out of flat paddocks, on the top of which a bush-ranger named Morgan had a lookout and a cave in our time.

A gum-tree grew there, and up that the Bunyip with his one eye climbed. At the foot the girl hesitated. She was afraid that she! could not climb well enough to scale so high a tree. To it came, panting and exhausted and suffering pain, the young man. And by that time it was night. The unfortunate lover was within a few paces of the object of his affections, and with his one eye he looked at her; but he also looked at the Bunyip. There he sat in the topmost branches of the eucalyptus tree, and he stared with his one eye, and his one eye and his staring fascinated the man.

He could not move. He, too, then came under the magic of the Bunyip, but he withstood it. No other blacks came near the place and there the three remained, until one day a storm came and blew down the tree, leaving the eye hanging in the sky. The Bunyip had died, and no one knew it. But now the man and the girl were freed from the spells, and they slowly returned the way they had come, and eventually found their people.

Their children are frog people, and they do not destroy frogs, leaving them to be food for the Bunyips so that those fearsome creatures may be appeased.

The eye left in the sky is the moon.

HOW THE WHITE WARATAH BECAME RED

There is really a white waratah.

It occurs in New South Wales and in Tasmania.

It is not a distinct variety unless we consider a flower a variety simply because of its colour.

The white of New South Wales and that of Tasmania are speciosissima and truncata respectively, though the plants always bear blooms of the colour even though they are in close proximity to those of the usual glowing red.

In Tasmania white waratahs are in some profusion. In New South Wales pink ones have been found, and they surely have in some way been impregnated. Occasionally the white ones have had a creamy tinge at the base of the pistils and in such cases the flowers have obtained some food that is usually the property of the foliage.

In New South Wales white waratahs have been found, and may still be found at Mittagong, at Sherbrooke and on the Jamberoo Mountain.

The natives of Sherbrooke had a legend of the changing of the white to red, and perhaps this story shows that it was believed that the first were white and the change to red was a later tffect. Of this we are not sure.

In the dense dark jungle there, a sleek and beautiful wonga pigeon lived. The rich soil in the gullied and sunken flats produced wonderful vegetation. Supplejacks and bloodwoods, cedars and monstrous turpentine! Great bushy lillypillies, overgrown myrtles, big laurels, towering eucalypts (E. Consideniana, the White Ash, E. Smithii, even E. Sieberiana, the Silver-top) shut out the daylight. Climbing plants grew there, with sweet smelling Sassafras (Atherosperma moschatum) and white Musk Daisy-bush (Olearia argophylla). In their shade the Flying Fox had camped for centuries unmolested.

Underfoot, the carpet of dark fallen leaves was feet thick. Down in there the horrible leech waved and swayed in his blind search for

40

an animal to fasten upon in order to get his fill of blood, while the brown bottle-tick lost no time in detaching himself from his habitat to bury his proboscis in some unfortunate passer-by, in the same quest as the leech.

In there, too, were gorgeous parrots and pretty pigeons and bower-birds, and tits and wrens, and such a host of the feathered tribes as to make them seem like a moving mass of wings and swaying feathers.

Big brush wallabies softly hopped or curled in a tangled bower; the bush rat and the bandicoot peeked from their seclusion, and the native cat slunk about as only felines can.

There, in this deep, dank, dark, sweet-smelling Australian jungle stepped daintily and cooed quickly and loudly, that proud wonga.

Sailing serenely up above it all were the hawk and the eagle.

While the wonga remained indoors she was safe.

Up over the cliff, where the country was flat, the bush was rocky and open and dry. A dryer air pervaded, the ground was no carpet of fallen leaves, but a hot, sandy or gravelled area with but few fallen leaves, for there was no underscrub.

The hawk's piercing eye saw every move there.

The white waratah gazed skyward and felt dreadfully alone. All around the waratahs grew and perhaps they were red, and this one was the only one without colour, and it longed to be crimson like its neighbours of its own botanical genus.

The handsome wonga had lost her mate. Her grey spots glowed against their bed of white; her little pink legs strode briskly on, and she scratched and scratched and turned up insects and grubs, and she fed well.

But when her thoughts turned to companionship she discovered that she was lonely. So she coo-ed and coo-ed, ever more and more rapidly, and in higher and higher tones.

She stretched herself upon tip-toes and searched the jungle. She ceased to look for a surfeit of food, and she stepped on and on, always approaching the creek where beyond it the cliff rose, and above it was the open forest.

Up out there she would go!

So she opened her wings, and, heavy as she was, she rose with a great and ponderous flapping.

Increasing her speed, she swept by the trees over the brook, and up the cliff, alighting just at the foot of the white waratah.

Then she heard the call of her mate.

Foolish bird that she was!

He was still down in the darkened jungle.

His morning could not have been so successful as hers, or he was hungrier to start with, or perhaps he required more.

She opened her wings again.

Too late!

A rush through the air, like a streak of lightning or a shooting star!

Swish!

The hawk was down through the branchless space and upon the beautiful wonga beneath the white waratah.

But she was heavier than he reckoned.

There was a struggle, and in it a whirl of feathers-white and grey and green and golden-shimmered!

The hawk certainly rose, but he did not carry the wonga far.

The pigeon was torn, and her life was ebbing with the flow of her blood. Her last struggle was her release, and from a height of a few feet she wrenched herself free and fell upon the white waratah. Her little claws grasped the colourless pistils.

The eagle above all espied the hawk, and he had then to fight another battle in which he was the loser.

So the white waratah was stained with the blood of the wonga pigeon, and the bird, still clinging to the reddened pistils, died.

Later, the white waratah threw out its clusters of follicles, and they were streaked with red.

The seeds were streaked in the same way.

And all the plants that came from them bore flowers as red as waratahs could be.

But they had to wait for three years to know that.

Not so the parent bush. Always afterwards its flowers were white, and whenever the natives saw one such bloom they pricked their fingers and allowed their blood to stain it.

Therefore there are not many white waratahs in New South Wales.

HOW THE SKY WAS LIFTED UP

According to the aborigines of Australia, the sky at one time in the ages ago was not up high where it is now.

It was down so low that a man could not walk upright. Then, no living thing stood erect. Everything either wriggled without legs at all, or crawled like a lizard or a goanna (iguana).

The reason that snakes and grubs and such like still crawl, is that the great event of lifting up the sky took place in the winter, and the creeping things were then hibernating. Birds that can fly through the air were most awake, and they followed the sky as it went up. In fact, they clung to it, and it was because of their beauty that they were allowed to sprout wings and soar back through the air. And they did that because of their hunger. There was no food up there.

The air itself was that part of the sea that clung to the sky and in falling was powdered, or vaporised, and still floats between the sea and the sky. The wonder to us is that it was not blacks who roamed the beaches and adjacent country that told the tale. It was the tribe that lived on the Murrumbidgee.

A great chief had a very beautiful wife. Though we do not really know, I am of opinion that her name must have been Krubi, for was not Krubi always the name of the most beautiful woman?

And this wife was the most beautiful in her day.

Well, the time for a corroboree had drawn near. Growing young men had not been initiated; that is, they had not been shown what to do in social, industrial, hunting and warlike things.

The beautiful wife of the chief was the one who fixed just where the women were to sit. She it was, too, who would give the signal when they were to retire, and she also was to be on the alert to hear the cry that meant they might come back.

No white man ever heard that cry. No white man ever saw a real corroboree, unless by accident, or more likely, stealth, and perhaps the aborigines were too finished in their bushcraft to allow that ever to happen.

43

The greatest secrecy was preserved. The keenest watch was kept, and all the whites ever saw was something of a mockery of a corroboree. The dance, even though a ceremonial one, was a different matter.

No native races ever kept their most sacred customs more hidden, nor were more cunning in disseminating false impressions of their real desires and real beliefs, than the Australian aborigines.

Now the place selected by Krubi (we shall call her Krubi) was condemned by the chief. He chided Krubi, and even threatened to cast her off for making the mistake of choosing an unsuitable spot. Krubi was piqued, and she retired to the gunyah, and there beat her breasts in dudgeon.

But her husband was her lord and she had to obey.

He ordered her to go out again and find a proper site, though he took care to indicate so pointedly as to practically tell her just where the best place was. The other women of the tribe knew what was wrong, and there were not wanting those who gloated over Krubi's discomfiture. So when one or two would have accompanied her Krubi waved them off.

She would go alone.

Now it chanced that another chief was not far away. He was a marauder, and he was on the lookout for game belonging to the Murrumbidgee people. Just as Krubi stepped upon a boulder in order to survey the spot this stranger came from behind the tree that hid him.

He was a good-looking black.

He gave the sign that his intentions were friendly and he walked swiftly towards the woman. He, she knew, was not "tabu." He was very far removed in blood. It was the men of the tribe who would have objected to his presence.

The women never concealed themselves from a member of another tribe. But they were supposed to report his presence.

Krubi did not intend to do any such thing. She had been humiliated before her other women. She was now out of tune with her husband. So she spoke to the stranger and asked him from whence he came. He seemed to not quite understand, so as a test of language he picked up a spray of gum-flowers that had fallen from a tree.

"Mannen," he said.

Now that was just what Krubi called it. It was the flower of the bloodwood or Eucalyptus corymbosa.

Then the man tried another.

He plucked a waratah and said, "Mewah."

44

The woman nodded.

Then said the man in his own rapid tongue: "I have come from far up on the hills," and he pointed up; "and I have not seen your people. Where are they?"

The woman, told him, and then she pointed to the creek just below.

"We shall go down there," she said.

So they went, and all the while the chief, who had gone into the gunyah to await his wife, grew more and more sullen.

At last he rose and strode out. Everyone backed out of his way for he had become very angry. He walked to the place he had indicated, and stood on the very stone upon which Krubi had stood to survey the place. He gazed all ways, and of course there was no sign of his wife. He jumped high in the air, and came down crash on dry sticks and leaves. Then he searched for the marks of his wife's feet. They were there. In one spot a displaced leaf, in another a fresh-broken twig. Even the flower of the bloodwood that had been handled he noticed, and he knew it had been picked up and thrown down again. There were broken umbels of the flower where it lay. There were broken stamens where it had been picked up. The chief searched around, and at last his eye lighted upon a little tuft of red fur. This was fur from the rock-wallaby, and Krubi had no such rug.

Neither had any of her tribe.

Passing quickly on be came across a foot-mark in a patch of soft, clear earth. It was the big imprint of a man's foot.

And there were, too, many broken twigs just around the fallen spray of bloodwood blooms.

He uttered the cry of battle. All the men of the tribe seized their war weapons and sped to him. Dogs barked, women screamed; children were dumb with terror. This was a sudden call to war! No corroboree so that the young men could be pressed into service! No preparation of any kind!

The need must be urgent; the trespass stealthy.

The chief gave his orders, and the tribe, relieved to find that no invasion in force had taken place, reassured the women and bade them await their menfolk without anxiety. The chase had commenced.

Krubi and her newfound mate had gained a big start. Their tracks were plain at first, but when they knew that they were followed they employed the arts and all the craft of their fathers. They broke off boughs and dragged them on their footprints. That was easily followed, but when they sprang sideways over a ledge of rocks and down into the stream, whether they crossed it or went up it or down it, was not easily determined. As a matter of fact, they went not any of these ways. They sank themselves in a pool and remained motionless, only their noses being above the water.

But before doing this they picked up stones and threw them over the other side, each one just a little beyond the other, so that the leaves and twigs were disturbed just as they would have been had they run there. It was some little while before any of the pursuers discovered the trick, and by that time the two had swum under the water and were at the far end of the hole.

And when we remember that the sky was so low that a man could not stand upright, but was stooped as low as a wombat, and when we visualise the bloodwood not more than a foot high which measurement was its girth and not height as we know it, we can see that all running, and all searching were infinitely more difficult than they are now.

Besides that, it was near to dusk when it began. It was now almost quite dark.

The pursuers gave it up. They knew very well that during the night the fugitives would go far, while they had to return to the camp to see their families; so they gave up all thought of ever catching Krubi or finding out with what stranger she went.

Not so the chief. He was determined to find his wife, and he was no less determined to punish the man.

Therefore, next day he chose one of his sons to act in his place, and he set out to succeed or die. For many days he travelled, and luckily he headed down the stream. Now and then he came across tracks that he felt sure were theirs.

One day he bethought him of the spirits, so he kept a good lookout in order not to miss any signs of the clay with which to draw the marks of the mysticism. Also he killed a white wallaby and plucked off all its fur. When he found the clay he drew the lines on his chest and body and legs, and by sticking the white fur in the clay he was in the proper dress. The Spirit came to him, and during the night he found out what lay before him. He had to follow the creek until it joined the river. Then he had to follow the river until it joined the great sheet of water. That sheet was either the sea or a very great lake. How far from the head waters of the Murrumbidgee the sheet of water lay we cannot guess, but from the manner in which the tale was told it seemed a very long way. It seemed to take longer than one man's life to get there.

But the blacks believed that the Spirit prolonged the lives at least of the three so that the wrong might be righted and the sky might be lifted up.

So the day came when the chief saw the two he was following.

They were camped upon the edge of the lake. No bloodwood grew there, but in the ages before other great trees had grown, only instead of standing upright, they grew horizontally. They were still there. And they were covered with age-long dried slime, showing that the water must have submerged them. They were in hundreds, thousands, millions. Lying about them and amongst them were great bones and great skulls, but everything showed that never had any one walked upright. The length of the bones of the arms showed that the animals had reached out and had crawled, and the shape of the feet, too, was such that they must have pushed themselves forward just as the ones written about were doing.

The chief did not hurry. He reckoned that he had them both at his mercy. There was plenty of food. Sweet roots abounded. Birds and animals were there, and besides, the lake teemed with fish and with molluscs.

The chief knew what was to be done. He chose a sharp stone and set to work hollowing out one of the great logs.

At last it was finished. He pushed it into the water. His wife and the other man saw him from where they lived, and guessing his intention to follow them into the water, they tried to escape by running along the shore and climbing in their stooped fashion over the logs. They soon came to an oozy spot. They could go no further along the shore for they sank deep and had hard work to get out, so they took to the water. They could not see across, but they chanced their power to reach the other side. Then the chief launched his log boat. He shoved it with an oar, and he shoved it so hard that the water rushed over the prow and filled it.

That he knew would not do. He would have to build something to prevent that, so he placed a frame in front that reached up to the sky (which was not high) and he wove twigs and rushes through and about it until no water could get through.

Then he tried again.

But still the water got in. It rushed around the sides of his shield. So he retraced his steps to where he had found the clay, and again he marked his body with the mystic signs.

He found this time that he had to get a certain rod that lay somewhere in the bottom of the lake. It surely was a rod made of gold, for the blacks say that it was very bright and of the colour of gold.

He did not search far before he found it. He lifted it up, and, behold! as it touched the sky, the sky went on and up before it.

And the rod grew. What a change took place then! Some water

47

left the main body and went up clinging to the sky. Birds that were accustomed to hanging to what was before the heavens were loth to leave it and they went up also.

'Possums clung for a little while and then let go. They to-day are the flying opossums and flying squirrels. So the sky went on up as far as the rod grew, and for as long as the chief pushed it. He was so awed at what he was doing that he forgot his quest-forgot to build the shield on the prow of the boat any higher, forgot that he only had wanted to rescue his wife and punish the marauder, and return to his tribe.

What became of the couple no one knows. Even what became of the chief and the rod no one is sure of. Whether they all died, and the rod, having done its work, sank back into the water, they can only guess at. They say that perhaps he is still somewhere pushing up the sky, and that it is when he grows tired and lets the rod down that the clouds cover the ground and fogs hide the world.

Perhaps, they say, that is the sky, and it only changes its colour from blue to white when it is again close to the ground.

Anyway, as soon as people found that they could stand upright they did so, and trees grew high and better.

The birds fly through the air because they could not go on up with the sky for want of food, and yet they do not wish to remain back on earth.

That is the story of the lifting up of the sky as told by the tribe of aborigines who inhabit a part of the head waters of the Murrumbidgee River.

THE FIRST KANGAROO

(Two Stories)

According to the inhabitants of the South-Eastern parts of the country-around the Monaro District, Mount Kosciusko, Goulburn, the Currockbilly Ranges, Mittagong, Burragorang and as far north as the Nepean River, there was a time when no kangaroos were in the land.

It is said by those people that the first kangaroo was borne to Australia upon the greatest wind that ever blew.

That wind came from the plains. It swept around the Macdonnell Range districts, whirling this way and that, careered back towards the north-western regions, across probably somewhere over Perth and Fremantle, swept over the Australian Bight, and finally blew out somewhere in Tasman's Sea. During all this terrible wandering and blowing the first kangaroo had a weary time.

He could not land. He was blown before that aimless wind and was tossed up and down. In his endeavours to gain a foothold his hind legs stretched out, and if they had not grown long as they did, he would never have alighted except in the sea, where he would have been drowned.

The chief was searching out new country. His tribe had cleaned out the particular spot where they had rested for many months, and game had become scarce. So the chief put on the paint that brought good luck, and sallied out to find a new and prolific pasture. He had travelled very many days without seeing a place any better, and was about to return to his people. But the little native bee which gathered pollen from the wattle just before him attracted his attention, and as he watched it he saw it dive down to a pool that lay in the black soil at the foot of the flowering tree. The black cautiously bent down, and with that dexterity which he possessed in a remarkable degree, he clasped, as he bent over the drinking insect, its wings between the forefinger and thumb of his right hand. He carried the bee to where he had noticed a hornet's nest, and detaching some of the cells of that, he moistened the substance, and stuck a little of it on the bee's back. Then he searched about for a cotton bush, and soon found one. The pods were bursting and the white balls were ready to fall. He stuck some cotton on the wax and released the bee. The strange feeling and the strange load caused the little insect to make a "bee-line" for home, and it was no trouble for the black to follow and keep it in sight.

On and on he went, never looking down nor to the right nor to the left, but always up, following the flight of the bee.

However, he was destined not to see the nest. Up in the sky something arrested his sight, and at once he lost the bee.

Indeed, he forgot it.

The strangest mass of cloud he had ever seen was there. It was sepia coloured with black edges. It seethed and curled and split. It billowed and curled and broke-and frayed out. Long spirals of lighter colour worked wonderful patterns against the brown, but drawing out and contracting, waving like giant battle-plane streamers, now straight as spears, now bent over like millions of boomerangs, now detaching, then adhering; the awe-striking masses of vapour came On from the west. Big rocks were tumbling there. Huge walls built up and tottered over and tumbled and crashed. Giant forests were born and waved in a giant storm and were felled. And with all that turmoil of vapour up aloft, the earth below was calm and serene. It faced an inevitable, and that inevitable was a catastrophe.

Suddenly it grew dark.

A night in the daytime descended in a second, blotting out everything. But in the heavens a wondrous light appeared. Long streams of liquid fire started from the south, and shot sheer across the heavens from pole to pole. They waved from west to east. Red and yellow, purple and brown, pink and grey, golden and black, white and pale green. All these colours in long straight fingers stretched from pole to pole, waved and crossed, and passed away towards the east. The unfortunate black man had never seen such a sight.

But he had heard of it.

It seemed to him that perhaps once in a lifetime a man was privileged to see such a thing. He cowered before it.

Then came the tornado. With the wind the lights waved out and the clouds passed, and the night (for it was really night then) showed starlight and clear.

But the wind roared on. Just above the trees a dull black shape passed over. It had long legs that hung down and clawed. The claws were not far above the black man's head. It was distinctly an animal. He could see the body and the neck, the head, the ears and the eyes, but in a few minutes it was gone.

Somewhere he seemed to know that it was food to eat. So he took heart. He really believed it was sent by the great spirit, for he was painted with the signs, and he was meat-hungry, and he was out, not on his own behalf, but searching for food for his people.

So he lay down to sleep, believing that in the morning he would find meat.

All night the wind blew. It was still blowing in the morning.

And he was so sure that it was to bring him some good thing that he moved not a yard.

The bees were again in the wattles. But he watched for the other creature.

It came.

It floated as before, being borne on the wind. The long legs still dangled and clawed. The black man followed. It led him an awful trip, but at last be saw it catch its claws in a tree-top and the wind passed over it and it fell. But like a flash it was up on its feet, and with great hops on those long legs it bounded through the bush and was lost to sight.

The chief returned. He retraced his steps. There were bees and birds, and there were many ferns which gave succulent roots. And seed-bearing grasses abounded. So to there the tribe moved their camp and they stayed for many a day. Now and then they sighted the new animal that had made its legs grow long by endeavouring to grasp the earth, but it was a very long time before it was speared. It must have caused a mate to come from somewhere, because the speared one proved to be young and others were seen. The flesh was good and the skin was covered with very warm fur.

Years afterwards someone found out how to tan it. The red blood-like kino of the bloodwood tree was soaked in water to dye the fur. A woman had wanted it dyed. The skin was allowed to be immersed in this coloured water for some days, and when it was removed not only was the fur dyed red, but the skin itself was changed. It was more serviceable. So ever afterwards those blacks soaked all their animal skins in a solution of this gum, and thus they tanned them.

Everyone had seen the aerial wonder, and they believed their chief had been answered by the Great Spirit and the kangaroo was sent from over the seas to succour them.

51

THE SECOND KANGAROO STORY

Away in the Kowmung and around the rugged peaks under which lie the great lodes containing the silver of Yarranderie, roamed a tribe of blacks who have their own tale of the first kangaroo.

These people said that one day a woman hid from her husband. This man was a very clever food-getter. His unerring boomerang brought down every goanna. The boomerangs that he fashioned for playthings only, would spin away out on their farthest boundary, and would return and spin again and again above the head of the thrower before swiftly landing at his feet, and that which he made as a weapon and, of course, would not return, was always the heaviest and most deadly, whether in hunting or in war.

He could deftly turn over the porcupine and could not miss a bird if he tried to bring it down. Therefore the bag of his wife was always filled with goanna tails, with great porcupines and birds and grubs, though the wife herself got the grubs as well as the fern roots. The grubs were the beautiful white ones that lie in interstices in old logs and are called "nuttoo."

The first kangaroo was said to be a great beast and was not innocent of eating small black children. Should a picaninny endeavour to crawl away from its rug or its sheet of bark its mother always threatened it with the calling of the giant kangaroo.

Now the heavily-laden wife one day rebelled. She threw away the heavy bag and ran off. She was fleet of foot, too, for no one could catch her.

Around that part of the country are many swampy patches, and these patches are mostly densely wooded with the Melaleuca Maideni and were similarly overgrown in the far-off days of the first kangaroo.

The fugitive wife hid behind the trunk of one of the biggest of these trees. Its bark is white, and in broad patches, soft and paper-like and irregular. It will peel off in huge scales.

Her husband often ran close to her, and she had to be very, very quick in her darting from the cover, and racing on.

52

Days went by and still she was not caught. But she was growing tired, and she began to think that carrying a heavy bag of tainted flesh was not so terrible a task as that of playing the grim game of hide and seek for life, in which she was obliged now to indulge continually.

Had she not been one of the women who had learned secrets that were supposed only to be possessed by the men, she would never have dared to rebel. If things came to the worst she could invoke the aid of the spirit, and something would happen in her favour. She knew where the necessary clay was to be found. The only trouble was that she was unaware of the whereabouts of her people. However, she chanced everything, and scaling the precipitous side of the mount she saw the smoke from the camp fire.

She was overjoyed to perceive that it was away towards the mountain now called "Werong," whereas when she escaped it was under "Alum Rocks." And between her and Alum Rocks was a deposit of red, and yellow, and white pipeclay. Thither she went, and soon she was correctly marked, and she even stuck the wild cotton in the lines of the clay to make sure that she would get the aid she needed.

By that time it was night, and she slept.

In the morning food came to her. The nuttoo grub poked its head from the trunk of the grass tree, and she had no difficulty in drawing him right out; and, roasted, he was very sweet. The taste of the nuttoo made her long for the grub that may nearly always be found in wattles.

It is well known that a very large number of very destructive insects inhabit wattles. The coolibah, too, is another host for pest grubs. And wattle and coolibabs grew in plenty, therefore in less than two hours she had collected a bagful, and then she sought a place to make another fire.

This fire was her undoing. The smoke was observed by her husband. He had never ceased to watch and to search for her.

With all his cunning he approached the little blue curling threads.

The woman was by no means unmindful. Her ears were alert, and distinctly she detected the distant crack of the broken twig, and the rustle o' disturbed dead leaves. The woman called upon the spirit, beating her breasts the while. Between her and the stealthily creeping man was a tea-tree stump. The top had been torn out by a gale and lay dead on the ground. She crept to it, and straightening up she clasped her arms around it, beseeching the spirit at the same time to protect and guide her.

The tea-tree stump became animated. It pulsed with life. It had almost parted from its roots before, for it was long since the branched top had been wrenched from it.

The man saw it quite plainly. It was only a tea-tree stump. The great flakes of bark were quite plain to him.

Therefore he did not watch it particularly. On he came until he could see the smouldering fire, and his nostrils told him of the cooking meal. There was no sign of his wife.

Well, he thought, never mind, this time. He would eat her meal and then he would spy out her tracks and follow her.

He passed within a few yards of the tea-tree stump, and just as he was quite off his guard and was about to begin the meal, the stump bounded off. He threw a glance up to it. Surprise held him paralysed. There, clinging to the stump as it went, was his wife.

He caught a glimpse of the white lines of the sign, and he gave up the idea of following.

Therefore ever since that time it is hard to tell a kangaroo from a stump. As he stands still in the bush one can easily imagine the black woman, plastered with clay and wild cotton, on his back. The dark forepaws of the kangaroo are her arms. His dark back is her body. His dark head is her face. But his white shaggy front is the ti-tree stump.

His one fault is his desire for black babies, and that was born of the woman who caused his being. Some believed that he ate them, but others deny that, and so they say it will never be known.

Even if not believed, the black mothers frightened their children by saying that he did.

THE STRUGGLE FOR SUPREMACY BETWEEN BIRDS AND ANIMALS

There was a time when Australian animals and Australian birds-the fauna and the avifauna-lived in the greatest harmony, and the thought of vieing one with the other to prove which was the stronger never entered their heads.

But a chief arose amongst the aborigines of the Megalong Valley who always set some one at variance with his neighbours, and, though he never went into battle himself, he caused many a war and much bloodshed. At last a time came when his people refused to quarrel at his behest.

The chief had one great gift. He could make friends with the animals and the birds just as easily as he could cause enmity between the people. He had one beautiful bird that was his especial joy. He taught it to mimic every other specimen of avifauna, and nearly every sound made by everything else. At that time all the other birds just sang or whistled softly, and the only animals other than the native dogs (which are not really Australian, any more than descendants of Irish, English or Scots can be) that made any cry at all were the native cats. The big tiger cats made a dreadful cry, the little spotted native cat miau-ed only; other animals simply murmured. The woolly native bear made no noise at all, and the cry he has now they say, is not his own, but is in imitation of something else.

One day a big tiger cat heard a cry. He took it to be the call of another cat. He answered it and strode through the scrub in search of the relation who uttered it. The sound seemed to come from directly ahead, but when the cat had searched the spot he was amazed and angered to find that the call of what he supposed to be a mate was behind him. Many times he went back and then forward, but all he could see was the chief of the black men and the chief's favourite bird.

He was afraid of that chief. He had many times seen the quarrels

55

and fights amongst the people who were spurred by him to kill one another.

During the searching the big striped cat met a wallaby. He told the wallaby of his dilemma. That animal had met the same thing. His soft murmuring and his occasional heavy grunt had been answered, but all he could find when he searched was the man and his brown bird with the perky head and sharp black eyes, and the wonderful tail.

Then the cat swore vengeance. He said he would follow the bird day and night, and one time or another he would kill it and eat it up.

So the cat fixed his attention on the man and his bird. He very soon found out that the man had taught the bird to mock all the sounds of the bush, and nothing delighted both of them more than to watch the fruitless searching of those they deceived.

One day he sprang upon the mocking-bird, and its struggles did not last long.

The black chief did not mind at all. He waved his arms gently, and purred and called in a strange way. His feathered friends came round him. He threw a nullah at the cat and killed it. He lifted up the clawed and torn mocking-bird and then showed anger, and the other birds became angry too. A pretty little native bear reared up its sleepy head to see what all the fuss was about, and shaking the youngster that clung to her back so that he might take a firmer hold, she slid to the ground. Another cat sprang upon the native bear (koala). The koala was terrified, and it was then that she first cried, for she had heard human beings cry when they were very frightened.

Up high in the branches of a tree sat a greenish bird. He had often heard the mocking-bird giving the calls and the sounds of the bush, and he tried to do it. He imitated the cat splendidly. In the cat's own voice he called it many terrible names, hiding the while behind a limb or crouching unseen in a deep fork. (The cat-bird now calls like a cat and hides behind a limb.) The vulture-crowned leather-head jabbered without ceasing and the chattering of that bird now is the remnant of the jabbering of that day.

A big brown and white bird-the kookaburra sat stolidly until he heard the cat-bird, and then he found that he could really be highly amused. His feelings found vent, and in the most wonderful way he laughed and laughed and laughed again. He enjoyed hearing the cat-bird calling just like a cat.

The kookaburra started the black and the white cockatoos. They screamed. They had never screamed before. They started the little robins and wrens and tits and shrikes, indeed, every bird in the bush. The clamour was awful.

The black chief who was responsible for all this hurled his spear. This was a signal for the rest of his people. They were standing awed or cowering in the thick scrub or behind rocks, but now they emerged and flung weapons, at intervals retiring to the cover again.

A boomerang that was flung stuck fast in the bark of a turpentine tree.

The din was added to when the birds attacked the animals. They had the advantage of being able to fly, and the animals were being defeated, but to their surprise they found that they could follow the birds by climbing. Even snakes wound themselves about small trees and climbed up.

Exhausted birds fell to the ground and were eaten by the sly cats that stayed to pick up just such dainties.

Darkness fell. Flying foxes were hanging to the big turpentine and they and the owls took but little notice of the disturbance until they began to move as is their wont when the daylight was disappearing before the blowing of the Big Man of the East. One big flying fox let go his hold and sank, only to be held by the boomerang that was fast in the bark. But that gave way and the huge bat, letting it go, spread his great leathery wings and sailed swiftly westward after the set sun.

While this struggling between the fauna and the avifauna was going on, and the black men of the tribe and the women and the children cowered again, more frightened than before, and the Bad Chief pretended to be as ignorant as they, the big flying fox reached the sun, and sank into it. A great shaft of light burst forth and returned to the earth. The birds and animals were blinded. They scurried down into dark places. So we have birds that can only see in the night. The sunlight blinds them.

There still are some wallabies and snakes and other ground animals that climb trees.

Also because a beautiful grey gang-gang was bitten by a cat and escaped, allowing some of its blood to stain the top of its head, we see the crimson crested gang-gang cockatoo. All other birds that remained alive, though bitten and bleeding, have now some crimson or pink feathers, such as the corella and the red head and others. Flowers that were below the wounded things and received some drops of their blood are tinged with red. The gang-gang fell into a great Doryanthes, and it is one of the reddest flowers of the bush. Before the bird died it crawled under a flowering burrawang. The seeds soaked up the last drops of blood and they are very red to-day. Drops fell upon the dainty epacris too, and upon the waratah. But there are other stories to account for the reddening of both these flowers.

The blacks of the Burragorang had a very beautiful story of the reddening of the waratah, and as they loved this bloom most of all, they told it often.

It is those of Tuggerall Lakes who told the pretty legend of the reddening of the epacris.

THE DIANELLA BERRY

We have given the rush with the pretty blue berries its name after the Goddess of the Woods—Diana—the hunter's deity. And it is strange but true that the aborigines had an idea much the same. They said that the plant at one time in the alcheringa was the hair of a certain woman who lived deep in the bush.

She had some sisters, however, and they lived sometimes in the forests and sometimes in the air for their other home was in the great cumulus clouds that lie lazily above the sea.

The one who lived in the bush only, had for a husband a mighty hunter whose voice was so loud that when he spoke angrily every animal and bird and even insect and reptile fled from that part of the country and did not return for a very long, time.

The woman was always most grieved when she saw the animals that she loved flying in fear, and one day when her husband had been especially angry one little bird grew too tired to fly far and it came to her for help. Her hair was at that time very luxuriant and she took the little bird and hid it in it.

After that many birds found the same sanctuary under similar circumstances and at last the number was so great that it was impossible for them all to be hidden. One bird-the woodpecker-begged to be allowed to leave and to try his luck by hiding under the loose bark of a big tree. This place was not secure, and when the angry man saw him there with part of his body showing, he threw his spear. It missed, but was so close as to make the woodpecker hop sharply further up. Another spear and then another were thrown, each one causing the frightened bird to jump one more step upwards.

The man's anger waned; his arm grew tired: he lay down to sleep. The bird flew to the woman and plucked one hair from her head. This he hid, hoping that the next time that the big hunter was angry and roared the hair would be enough to cover, not one woodpecker only, but the whole woodpecker family.

59

It is noticed that woodpeckers to this day hop up and up the trunks of trees and the blacks say that they are looking for a place to hide from the wrath of a forest giant. They listen intently and strain their ears to catch the sound of the roaring.

We know that the birds are simply looking for food, and some of us believe that the aborigines know this quite well, only feigning to think that it is for any other purpose. Perhaps they think the tale is too pretty to lose.

Next time that the hunter was angry and threatening, the woodpecker tried his plan. He flew to the place where he had hidden the strand of hair, and he found that he could be covered with it by winding it around himself until none was left hanging. Other birds saw the plan and followed it.

The time came when the woman had but little hair left. But rain fell where the hairs were put and warm sun shone on the places and the hairs grew and flowers came upon them all and afterwards berries formed.

It was no longer necessary for the birds and the animals to flee far to escape the wrath of the husband of their benefactor.

They only had to quickly haste to one cluster of growing hairs and snuggle down in amongst them and they were quite hidden.

But the day came when a jealous sister came down from the cumulus cloud. She told the man and he declared that he would find every one of those clusters and destroy them. The sister gave directions to the rest of the family still up in the sky that they were to keep their clouds away from the place so that no more rain could fall and the hairs would no longer grow. She saw that the wife was now denuded of hair and she wanted to please the husband and thought that no more could ever be seen after those growing ones were destroyed.

But the berries had fallen and lay covered by the now dry soil. The clusters of hairs did die, and the earth suffered from a great drought.

Then the man grew more and more sullen and was more and more often dreadfully angry. His wife had gone away from him. The birds had hidden her and with their wings they protected her, and the cloud sister lived in her place.

She no longer spoke to those still in the sky. They heard of her treachery and they did not want to speak to her. They at last determined to no longer heed her request to keep away from that place and they came again and they brought the lightning and the thunder with them. They poured their rain down upon the earth and every little blue berry gave birth to another hair that took root and became a plant.

The rain kept on longer than ever before and there was a great flood, but not any of these hair rushes was destroyed. To-day they grow where the ground is wettest, as well as in dryer parts.

Aboriginal women of all the east coast of Australia know this story and they believe it, and because they think that the spirit of the woman who loved birds and animals is still in the dianella rush they like that plant best for the weaving of baskets and mats.

HOW THE PISTILS OF THE WARATAH
BECAME FIRM

Of all the flowers in our Austra one which was most revered by the blacks (in fact the only one so far as we know) was the watarah. No other flower was ever sufficiently noticed by them to be plucked and given, or shown, to whites, with a sense of gratitude for a good done to them.

There was a time, say the natives of the Burragorang Valley, when the waratah was not as we see it to-day. The pistils were soft and downy, and when the wind blew they fell off and floated away like the thistledown.

It all happened at a corroboree.

Wantaba and Wirrawaa were rivals for a maiden. Both men knew that he who sprang the highest in play, he who wielded the longest spear, and above all, he who went out alone into the dark and brought back the finest 'possum or the prettiest flower plucked in the dark of night, would win the girl.

The hated and feared tribe that came over the hills from the swampy country at the base of the great unscalable mountain had twice been seen trespassing on the Burragorang side of the waterfall, and two corroborees had been held so that the young men who had never had a fight might be shown how to hurl a spear and how to crouch, and how to wield the millah, and dodge a blow, and also how to feign death if the enemy hit hard enough and proved to be too strong.

The warriors, old and new, sallied out, and climbed to the top of the Dividing Range. There they sat around little pools of rain water that the tiny basins in the rocks held, and rubbed and rubbed their stone axes and spearheads, and chanted song after song, deriding the wrongdoers of the other tribe, until at last one of them yelled to know what all the din was about.

The answer was a hurled spear. Wantaba was anxious to show what he could do, and he threw the spear that had taken him many days to fashion. Wirrawaa was more cautious. Plucking a waratah, which was then only a soft cluster of pollen like a wattle, he held it before his face while he took a careful aim at the seeming valiant enemy. He moved carefully forward, crouching the while just as old Wollayabba had done at the corroboree in which he was the teacher of the warlike arts, and knowing that by the time he was near enough to be sure of killing the foe and recovering, too, the spear that he would soon fling, many others of the opposing force would be collected at the spot.

He drew nearer the edge of the ridge, step by step, and then came a puff of wind. The fluff of the flower blew back into his eyes, and just then came a spear from the throwing stick of one of the foes.

Crack! It caught Wirrawaa fairly on the forehead, and down be went like a stone.

That was the signal for a rush. Fighting men of both sides had clustered in rear of their companions, and now came the deciding clash.

Down below on the sides of the ridge and on the top of another the women and children waited and watched and listened. Some could see the battle, some were too frightened to look, and some were not allowed to see what was going on. They could all know by the nearness of the noise which side was giving way, and the Burragorang women grew much afraid. They gathered up their mats and bags, for the sound of the fighting grew ever louder.

Their men were being fought back. There were some bark shields lying handy, and two or three of the girls who had lovers fighting up on the hill grabbed them and rushed nearer to the fray. Wantaba, who had thrown the first spear was still in the battle line. Just as the girls with the shields came in sight, Wantaba received a mighty blow from a kurri, as the knobbed fighting-club was called.

He turned and fled. Catching sight of the young woman for whom he and the fallen Wirrawaa strove he saw that she was holding out a bark shield for him, and he sped to her.

But she asked for Wirrawaa. Wantaba pointed to his own head and then to a point in the midst of the struggling warriors and returned to the fray. The girl was afraid now that he would be killed like Wirrawaa, so calling to Wantaba she too rushed into the fight, and just in time.

Many of her people had thrown down their clubs. Most of them were either killed or badly injured.

But when the survivors saw a woman laying about her with an old stick, and warding off blows with a man's huge bark shield, they

63

picked up their weapons again and fought more determinedly than ever.

They won, and the trespassing blacks were driven far into their own territory.

Upon the return of the pursuers to the scene of the fight a procession was formed in which were a few young women, and this was an unprecedented thing. There was a triumphal march back to the camp and the place was cleared for another corroboree.

Wantaba was asked to tell his story and, dressed for the part in his proper war colours, he acted it and pointed out the girl who had fought and acclaimed her the real conqueror.

Then at the end of this recital and this portrayal the women were all sent into thick scrub, and Wantaba was inducted into the mysteries of the marriage state.

But the ceremony had to be postponed for the girl was not to be found. She had disappeared and no one had seen her going. When daylight came the whole tribe engaged in the search, for it was believed that she could not possibly have gone far, and it was feared that she had received some hurt.

She had entered again into the domain of man, for she had communed with the god of her totem. She had asked that Wirrawaa be allowed to come back from the spirit world to her. She had taken a waratah and had shown how the fluffy bloom had succumbed to the blowing of the wind and had proved no protection to a fighting man. And her prayer was answered. Wirrawaa came back, though a much changed man. His skin was white and the eyes that before were nearly black were now sightless and blue.

And he had a strange power. He could alter the form of trees and change their flowers. As a protection to any other fighting men who might pluck a flower or a plant when going into battle, he caused spikes and thorns to grow upon many trees and he changed many soft flowers into hard ones. The waratah became the firmest of all.

The prickly hakea now prevents any one from pushing through it. Smilax and many other vines produced such thorns and prickles that they were a sufficient guard to any lands.

For a long time it was believed that no spear would go through a waratah flower, and many blacks would ask white men to put one up and let someone hurl a dart or a spear and it would not go through. So much faith was placed in that, that many men would not go into battle without a waratah if they were in flower at the time of the quarrel.

64

WHAT MAKES THE WAVES

Arrilla was of the Kamilaroi.

He lived principally on the coast, not far from our present village of Coal Cliff-between that and Stanwell Park.

Perhaps he was not any real individual, but only a type-creation. Be that as it may, all that is ascribed to him in this legend is what happened under the circumstances delineated. The story was told as being of one particular man, and yet there is that in the telling of it that seems to indicate a wish to show tradition rather than tell of the actual doings of one person.

He was the cleverest of his tribe.

He was not afraid of the sea.

He roamed as he willed over his country, and even when enemies appeared on the top of the range and a hurried council was called by the King, Arrilla did not hasten to obey the summons if he happened to be studying the inhabitants of the sea, or the denizens of the creeks that came clattering down the slopes and spread out into beautiful lagoons on the beach.

For his country is a narrow strip of sub-tropical country, backed by a jungled range with ironstone scarps for its topmost face scarred by cold creeks and edged by bold promontories and yellow scalloped beaches that bound the limitless expanse of Pacific Ocean.

He never dared to remain away from a summoned council altogether.

And one morning when the sun shone calmly and clearly down through the blue, and the mountain was purpled, and the lower slopes were deep green and dark with the jungle, and the strip of undulating land that lay between it and the beach was bright with the semi-tropical verdure such as the tamarind, and the Archontophoenix and Livistona palms, and the giant Alsophila ferns-Cooperi and australis-and the promontories stood with their shaggy westringias and hibbertias and hardenbergias and white button-flowers all aglow, staring, staring, staring out over the blue

65

lazy ocean, and casting blue and purple shadows across the yellow sand of the beach, even reaching to the masses of white foam that were swept ashore, when the little breakers were dashed to pieces, the enemy was seen on the top, above the dark wall of ironstone, right out on the edge, waving spears, and he was heard shouting to the family of Arrilla down on the beach.

The voice carried far.

Aborigines could be heard at a distance of seven miles.

They made hollows with their hands, and the coo-ee that rang through them was a wonderfully penetrating and floating call.

The King was young.

It was not long since his father was laid in the shallow grave that was scooped out in a grassgrown sandhill.

The spears were buried with him.

They put him sitting with his face towards the mountain and his knees doubled up to his chin and his arms crossed over his stomach.

His three wives still sat and beat their breasts in grief, and the blood that ran from the cuts they made in their thighs was dried on their legs, for they would not wash it off for three moons.

The young King was as stern as his father had been.

He was as straight as a rush, too, and he was fleet and wary.

Above all, he was determined.

So when Arrilla delayed he ordered two strong men to go to the lagoon and seize him.

Now Arrilla was cunning.

He had practised his subtleties on the old King, and that is why he was allowed to respond to a summons as unhurriedly as he wished.

Arrilla asked to be allowed to speak, and the permission being given, he drew himself erect and waited until he saw that the expectancy of the warriors of the family was beginning to make them impatient.

Then he pointed to the highest spot on the range. He told them that in his wanderings there he had seen a spirit. The spirit was not friendly to him, but would be good to any stranger who came over the range at that point. He said that the enemy that then stood on the very spot was receiving his courage from that spirit and there was only one way to overcome it.

It was not by an organised battle. It was by strategy, and he was the only fighting man of the family who possessed the cunning.

And in that way Arrilla tried to palliate the King and to escape the opprobrium that always attached itself to those who disobeyed or were dilatory in answering a call to the councils or an order of the King.

But this time the King was not convinced. He said that the meeting was to be adjourned until night came, and then the further evidence of Arrilla would be taken. There was, he said, no immediate danger from the enemy above. If he were prepared to fight he would have been down before, said the King. He was only seeking to make the people below too angry to fight, and then he might bring his forces down and get the gain he was after.

So the meeting broke up. Arrilla was free. That much he had gained he knew, for he saw very plainly that though he had been always before successful in placating the King, this time he was in deep disfavour and perhaps would be punished.

He had succeeded in making his fellows think he had had communion with a spirit on the top of the range, and with them that belief gave him a great prestige. All aborigines were vain and fond of power, and in that they were no very great amount different from white people.

Arrilla went to the wurley of his wife, and for a little while he played with his two children.

Then he looked into the dilly-bag, and finding that there was not much in it, he decided to go out in search of some food. He had noticed women putting things within reach of his wife, but he had been too busy with his own interests to see that his larder was so empty.

Taking up a spear and a shield he strode into the scrub. There was, at first, a thick tangle of boronia-Boronia mollis-and its scent was not pleasant to him. Bracken fern, rank and tall, Chorizema and snake vine, Bauera with the always blooming pink flowerets, and Tetratheca, with the layer of tangled twigs, made the going difficult. Prickly wild raspberries made the way even more hard for him. Then he entered the dark jungle itself. Its edge was a mass of myrtles interwoven with the rubus and flowering tecoma and clematis. These vines lay thick on the top of lantana, and through them grew up the Lillypilli and Rapanea and the fluffy-flowered Callicoma. Xylomelum pyriforme or native pear trees with their wooden fruit and unpleasant odour, and the Goodenia ovata with its dark serrated leaves and yellow flowers and the Pittosporum and Sassafras were all clasped together and held close by native jasmine, and up through it all the cabbage and bangalow palms and the Eucalyptus microcorys or tallow wood and the Swamp Mahogany or robusta of the eucalyptus genus stood into the humid air.

Big cold boulders were lying undeil the deep shade of the scrub and ferns and the clustered true and false sarsaparilla, and they were covered with moss and lichen, and attached to them were dendrobiums and big aspleniums or bird's-nest fern.

It was always dark in there.

The lyre-bird darted under the thick moss and the carpet of Randia and tiny wild violets overlaid with the tough and thick-leaved Smilax australis.

Its nest was placed on a flat ledge of the biggest rock and it had in it a furry youngster that sat as still as the rock itself, its eye of black fire fully taking in the cautious Arrilla.

Right in front the mountain reared, still clothed with the jungle, with giant rocks fast to the sides, and the vines, especially the tough monkey vines, clinging to big gums-the turpentine, the woolly-butt, and the spotted gum and the wild fig with its mass of roots between which men could hide and wallabies often had their lairs.

Arrilla sought the wallaby. The rufus-necked scrub variety was in plenty here. Arrilla only had to stand still with poised spear and an unsuspecting marsupial hopped into view.

"Swish"!

It was like a dart of lightning.

Then Arrilla "twooped" like a beautiful wonga pigeon, and he whistled like the king parrot, and those birds came to what they supposed was a calling mate.

He very soon had a fine collection of game for his food and the meat of his family. He was a snake man and only reptiles were tabu to him.

It grew night again.

The rest of his people were scattered about on the clearer and lighter land, nearer the beach-some idling and some fashioning weapons. Some indeed were making cradles, but not on rockers as are our cradles. They had strings attached and could be fastened round the neck of the mother.

A few had made a poison from the acacia for their fishing, and yet others were wading in pools in the rocks seeking mussels and shell-fish.

Beyond, the lazy sea just heaved and sparkled and sent its messengers of breakers to be broken on the sand.

By this time a black band had spread along the horizon, for night was approaching.

What had become of the gesticulating blackfellow on top of the range no one knew.

No cooking fires were lighted. Little heaps of sticks lay about-all gathered by the fathers and the children. Suitable stones were collected too, but the order had gone out that everyone must eat either raw or cold food, and a big council would be held on the low, flat, grassy patch down near the lagoon.

Only after nightfall did the sea begin to moan.

The little crash of the breaking waves in the daytime was quite cheerful, but in the darkness it seemed to ring with a different tone- one of sadness and pessimism.

The council sat in the dark. Only the fighting men and the priests were in it after all.

Arrilla was there.

The discussion did not last long, and it all centred upon the tale that Arrilla had told.

He was a frightened Arrilla when he found that he was expected to climb to the highest point of the range and ask questions of the spirit to whom he said he had spoken.

He dared not disobey.

When the meeting was over and the men had retired to their wurlies and their families, Arrilla sat for a long time arranging in his mind how he would proceed as soon as it was light.

He determined not to go by the way he had gone before. He would go a long way round.

He knew of a gully up which it was easy to climb and which would allow him to approach the enemy by a flanking manoeuvre, and then he could spy upon him and perhaps use his spear.

So in the morning he said "good-bye" to his wife, and having received a sacred stone from the priest for placing in his hair above his ear for good luck, he again crossed through the boronia and leptospermum and bracken undergrowth, and entered the jungle. He went to the rock on which was the lyre-bird's nest, and then turning to the right he passed close to a giant nettle tree and a Stenocarpus, and that way the going was easy. He was still under the big trees and hidden from anyone's sight unless someone were very close.

The scent of the dendrobiums came to him, and as he passed lilly-pillies he broke off a few clusters of the white and juicy fruit and ate them. He picked up ripe and luscious black apples, and here and there he gathered the little red berries of the Rubus parvifolius. The wild raspberry he made a detour for, but it was not growing in that part. Occasionally he tore up a leaf from the bird's-nest fern and at the end there is a crisp and succulent part which he chewed.

He reached the upper part of the creek that formed the lagoon down below on the beach, and as he was gradually ascending the lower slope and using the maximum of precaution, he came to a spot high on the mountain side from which he could look out through the branches and over the heads of the tall shrubs and high gums to the sea.

The sun was well up and the morning was becoming warm.

The sea was still lazy though a little glitter on its surface showed that it was under a disturbance, slight enough, but discernible.

Then he turned his back to that view and the climb proper commenced. It was steep. He hoisted himself by grasping the stems of the callicomas and the rapaneas and the myrtles that grew sparsely here, and sometimes he was lucky enough to find a monkey vine hanging to a tree and that gave him a splendid lift. Though he was somewhat afraid of his errand and quite alone, he was not anxious to lose time; yet the temptation to swing on a monkey vine was too strong, and finding one that had a big loose bight in it he seized it and pushed himself off with his feet. Out he swung over the steep side and above the undergrowth and through the lesser limbs of the Pittosporum that grew just beneath, and then he had a clear and uninterrupted sight of the country at the base, and of the beach and the sea. The vine gave a little twist and returned, and the swing was exhilarating.

But he only did it once, and letting the vine go he faced the escarpment and went on with his climb. He secured precarious footing on the stones and exposed roots and in the moss. Sometimes a loosened stone went bounding and crashing down until it struck the foot of a tree and lodged there.

Arrilla now looked up. He had reached a spot where the big trees did not grow, and the only verdure was rock fern and dianella rush with its tiny blue and yellow flowers and its blue fruit.

Above him the blue sky was unclouded and a great lazy sea-eagle floated serenely.

He had disturbed many birds in his climb. The coach-whip had darted from him. The wonga pigeon and the little brown fantail and the woodpeckers and the honey-eaters and the diamond sparrows and white-eyes and silver-eyes all had paused to watch him go by. Satin birds and catbirds and parrots sat in the branches or darted through them as he passed under, and in the wild figtrees the beautiful flock and topknot pigeons clattered and scrambled for fruit.

A small colony of flying foxes hung like a giant swarm of bees in a fire-tree, but Arrilla did not see them. This fire-tree is a Brachychiton, and it is of the same genus as the Queensland bottletree. It sheds its leaves and its brilliant flamelike flowers cover the twigs and blaze out before any of the new season's leaves come.

It is rightly named "fire-tree," though some people call it "flame-tree," and apply this—name also to the Erythrina or coral tree of Queensland.

He was in the narrow cleft, between the sides of which the water raced in rain-time, and he was near to the top.

When reached it, and before he had climbed over the ledge, he was in a bracing upper air. The verdure, he could see as he peered, was different. The Epacris and the Boronia pinnata and Boronia serrulata, and also Star-hair made a pink carpet.

Arrilla was out of breath and perspiring when he heaved himself over and stood upright in that upper air with its scents of new flowers.

On damp and mossy and heathy patches the Blandfordia bloomed. On drier parts the false sarsaparilla or Hardenbergia monophylla clambered over the stones and boulders and clefts, and hung its blooms in purple clusters.

Here and there a big yellow Podolepis acuminata glowed and the white fur from the stems was detached and lay on the ground.

Box-trees-the Eucalyptus bicolor-and stunted Banksia serrata, and Callistemon lanceolatus tried to find sustenance.

Mustering all his caution Arrilla advanced along the edge of the mountain. Heath abounded, hard rock-fern clustered thickly, stunted callitris scrub, Olearia or mountain musk' dwarfed eucalypts, honey-flower or Lambertia formosa, little casuarinas, wild currants, or Leucopogon richei and bracken fern, were matted with kennedya, well out in crimson and black flowers, and here and there rising through them stood the gorgeous crimson waratah.

As Arrilla quietly crept along the edge he could see down over the verdure to his people near the beach, and he noticed that many were looking anxiously in the direction of the point on which he had seen the enemy native the day before.

He had all their love for the representative flower of his race-the waratah-and he plucked one in order to render himself immune from fire should that occur.

Suddenly he cast himself into a rigid statuesque figure of a man.

He heard the breaking of twigs and the footfall of someone. He moved not a muscle. His spears were in the hand that held the shield.

The noise ceased.

Then the air darkened. There were no clouds, but a great deep shade spread all over the earth.

Arrilla looked to the sun.

It was disappearing.

He grew mightily afraid.

He had almost persuaded himself that he really had spoken some time or other to a spirit up there, and this terrible fading out of the sunlight came to show that he was even then trespassing on the country of it. The place surely was sanctuary and tabu.

So making the sign with his hand that he had seen the priests make he softly whispered a magic word.

The strange shade grew rapidly deeper and then Arrilla became conscious that another aborigine was standing just as frightened as he and was looking at him fixedly.

Arrilla made a friendly sign and the other advanced. He was an utter stranger but his language was much like Arrilla's. They could well understand one another.

He told Arrilla that he was in country strange to him, and his story was a long one. He had never before seen the sea, and he did not know what it was. He believed it to be a great sky, and beyond it there was, a very bad country. He said that the sky had fallen down and that it was slowly creeping on and on and eventually would cover the whole world. In his country he had heard some such tale about it. It was that a great ancestor had left the earth and had gone up into the sky. He went so fast that he drove right through it and he had seen the very bad country that is beyond it. He tried to return but the hole that he had made was closed up. Yet he did not give up hope, and by beating upon it he loosened it and it fell. It had as much life as a man, and it very much wanted to return from whence it had fallen. The ancestor was always with it, floating upon it. And when it tried to rise up to return the ancestor beat it back and it could do nothing but sink down and break itself on the beach. However, it was surely growing and spreading, and the time must come when it would cover the earth.

He had heard all these things and he had determined to see for himself, and that is why he had made the journey in the direction his people had pointed out as the one where the great sky lay.

Arrilla was delighted to hear this story. Though he had been born near the sea and lived there all his life he had no story of what it is, nor how it comes to be there, nor why the waves beat on the shore.

He advised the strange man to wait until he had gone back and communicated the news to his people, and said that when the signal fire was made he might come down and be received by the King. But Arrilla told him to say that a spirit gave him all this information about the sea and the waves, and that while it was being told Arrilla was present.

Both forgot their fears of the strange darkness that had come over, and down below his people still wondered what had caused it. They thought it was because Arrilla had met the spirit and was talking to it, and as the shade passed and the sun came out bright again and the gladness that is usual to the sunshine spread again all were in high glee. There was nothing wrong, they said, and Arrilla would return with news and the spirit he had seen and spoken with would assist them if they had to fight with any trespassing tribe or family group.

Soon after Arrilla joined his people again, having come down the way he went up, and he told the story of the sea as he had heard it from the stranger, though he said it was told him by the spirit.

Fires were lighted, and when the man came to them he said he was very hungry, and he told the story just as Arrilla had.

A wife was found for him from amongst the women-girls and he lived there for the rest of his days with that family.

The sea grew rough when the wind blew, and he said that he had heard that that was the impatience of the sea. It was angry and impatient because of the great delay occasioned by the ancestor who refused to let it go back to where it had fallen from.

The roar is the voice of the ancestor who always refuses to go back. When the calm came again it was because the sea was worn out and very tired, but nothing could stop it from ever creeping further and further over the land. The winds, be said, were the spirit friends of the sea, and they tried to assist it to regain the place that it had lost.

The Kamilaroi people always believed that the day would come when the sky would go back and the earth would be quite dry and life could not exist, but they were not afraid, for they said that the day was yet a long way off.

THE FIRST BUSH FIRE

One of the pioneers of the Goulburn district lived near Taralga. He was an old Scot and he knew the aborigines. He was a lover of flowers and a man who learned to respect the blacks. He wrote nothing; he said but little. Very few of his friends knew that he had such knowledge of the bush and its people.

Some of the stories in this book came from him. His son Alex got them, and even Alex kept them to himself for a long time. No one in the Burragorang Valley knew more than Alex of the stories of the natives, and few were better able to control the remnant of the once powerful tribes when they had learnt vice and cunning from the whites and became troublesome. The vice of the white and his cunning when added to the cunning of the black made a vicious compound, and for many years that compound is all that has been seen of the nature of our autocthonous predecessors.

Beneath it is still the gentleness and the softness of heart of these black people. These beautiful attributes were always below the surface, but if a white has the gift of sympathy and the spirit of understanding they rise to the top and the black is seen in another light.

Alex. sat on wild, wet, cold, winter nights before the fire with his mother. His father was still away somewhere on the rugged run with his cattle and with his black friends. Sometimes his staying away lasted for more than weeks, but never were Alex. and the mother unduly anxious for they knew that the blacks would lose their own lives if necessary to save that of their white friend. Then when the father returned he would sit at the fire too, and he would tell of what he had seen and what he had done, and always in the stories would be the mention of his companions-the blacks. Their legends as told were retold. Their beliefs, as they could be gauged, were recounted. But Alex. did not know their importance and he did not write them nor did he remember all of them.

This is one of a bush fire.

There was a time when the Australian bush was different from what it is to-day. Trees were bigger and their wood softer. There were more and bigger and brighter flowers. And the land-especially the mountains-was far more densely clothed with verdure.

But some change came, and it was not good for the land. Seeds failed to germinate, and where fertile tracts had been now desert appeared.

Somewhere away in the south, perhaps away over in Victoria, there lived a great king. His people were very numerous, for he had imposed his will upon other tribes than that which was his when he was first made ruler, and he had succeeded in welding them all together into one harmonious group. They revered him and all sorts of presents were laid by them at his feet.

Yet he never shirked work, and he took a place amongst the hunters just the same as if he were not a king. He must have come as far north as the Burragorang—if, indeed, he had not come further—for the Hunter River people have a story just like this.

Living in a valley between two mountains was a very small tribe-an unusually docile people. They were an offshoot of that tribe who owned the country at the head of Cox's River. The Powerful chief heard of them, and he determined to find out what they were like and add them to his subjects. So he set out by stealth.

Wrapping himself about with a wombat skin he came to the hiding-place. He was a very big man and he could not well conceal himself in so small a skin as that of a wombat-even the biggest of them. Therefore when he was within sight of the camp he hid behind a rock. He saw that the tribe were very busy just at the time cooking game by heating stones and placing them one after another around and upon the carcases. The handling of the stones was made easy by the wrapping of waratah stems about the fingers.

This wrapping of waratah stems to make a person immune from burns was so believed in by the blacks that they came to the first blacksmiths that they saw and offered them the twigs, indicating that if they would wear them no flying sparks could injure them.

Now amongst the people was one maiden of exceptional beauty. Some say that the reason for these blacks ostracising themselves was that many years before a beautiful woman wished her pretty baby to be called Krubi, and the other Krubi was not yet old. So the mother gathered her children about her and went away, and the family increased and increased, and always there were those quite beautiful enough to be called by the coveted name of Krubi.

But again it might have been because of the social system as explained in another legend that any portion of a tribe went further afleld and formed another and distinct group.

Anyhow, when the king saw this maiden he lost all his cunning, so entrancing was she, and jumping up without reserve he ran towards the people. They started up in fear and scattered in many directions. The king called to them not to fear him, but she did not understand his speech. The beautiful maiden soon found that the stranger pursued her, and her alone. She was very fleet of foot and very cunning, and by dodging and crouching she eluded him. Sometimes she was so close and so still, standing beside a tree, that he ran past her, and only by not hearing her crashing through the bushes and stamping on the twigs and leaves did he know that he had gone too far. No sooner did he turn than she bounded off again.

There was a stream clattering down a gully and falling over boulders and ledges into pure cold pools, and towards that stream the girl now ran. She knew of some footholds close to a waterfall, and, indeed, sometimes even behind it, that led to a very large and deep pool, and outstripping the now panting king she reached it. Never hesitating she clambered and swung herself down, and reaching the bottom she swung over the last ledge and slipped into the water.

The king reached the top of the fall, and believing that his quarry could not have gone down there he retraced his steps. He went right back to the camping place and found it, of course, silent and deserted. So he returned to the people he had left and told nothing of where he had been and what he had seen.

As often as he could he went back, and though sometimes he saw some of the people, never did he catch sight of the girl. He went so often that the others grew not to fear him. They guessed his desire, and they aided the girl at all times to hide from him.

One day he overlooked the people who were unaware of the fact that from a neighbouring eminence the king could see them. They had grown so careless that they did not think of pitching their mia-mias where no one could see them from a distance.

And he caught a sight of the maiden of his desires. But she saw him and once more she had to run as if for her life. He did not hurry after her. Instead he got two dry sticks, and sharpening one on a stone he placed the flatter of the two on the earth before him, and putting the point of the other on it he rubbed and twisted it round and back between his palms until he had caused a fire to glow. He had dry ferns and grass ready, and placing them on the glowing spot he gently blew until the flame burst out. He added more fuel until he had a big blaze. The wind blew in the direction of the little tribe, and soon a great roaring fire was leaping and leaping and shooting out curling masses of consuming flame.

The girl saw it coming. The tribe saw it also. Away they all ran, bounding and crashing, but the fire came faster. It overtook some of them and they perished. On the blackened cleared ground the now wicked king followed. But he could not go fast. The smouldering sticks and rubbish were still hot. There were no waratahs growing just here for the waratah does not grow as profusely as, say, the gums, but in patches far apart. Hot as he was and suffering burns as he was still, he examined every body he came across, but they were none of them the one he sought. A last he came to two little heaps of clay. What was this? These heaps told to him a story. They were fresh. They were composed of the clay that the tribal doctor used to make the mystic markings, and the tribal priest used for the same purpose when he wished to invoke the aid of a Great Spirit. Who had used it? Not once had he seen anyone who looked like one who had been initiated into the doubly-hidden mysteries of the rite that gave power to invoke the Spirit. Surely the girl had not seen that corroboree. If she had, then not only could he never capture her, but he was himself lost.

And lost he surely was. For on looking behind him he found that almost as the fallen seeds of the trees were being consumed by fast or slow smouldering, they were bursting with new life, and plants were springing up in such profusion as to block his view.

In what direction had he come? Which way would he turn to go back? The smoke was so dense that he could not see the sun. The trees that lay over from the prevailing winds and gave some idea of direction were burning, and their small branches were gone.

Surely, he thought, this is the work of the maiden and she knew more than any woman was allowed to know.

He wandered on and on, the bush growing denser. He stayed sometimes to pick up something to eat, for burned and roasted game lay in his path, and succulent roots were cooked. He wandered for many days quite lost.

The girl had visited at night the tribe from which her family was an offshoot, and had come across the corroboree that taught her how to paint herself, and this she had done, and the charm was hers.

A new camping place was chosen by the few who escaped that terrible fire, and the year rolled away. The young plants flowered and their seeds fell, but the next year no new plants came up. This was noticed and talked about by all the people. Even on the river where a few of her people were now living no seeds sent out the little plumule nor their little radicle, and no new plants grew to grace the world with fresh flowers, nor to produce the roots nor fruits for food.

Again the maiden thought of beseeching the spirit. She went back to the old ground all alone and she found the clay. She painted herself and awaited results. She heard the spirit and she talked with it. Then she noticed that just before her a little smoke wreath curled up into the air. Then a flame burst, and in a very little while a fierce bush fire was raging.

The girl was satisfied that a fire was what was needed and she sent word to the river to say that all would soon be well with the world. That the seeds would germinate and new plants would grow up and flower and all would be gay as before.

Since that time bush fires do not need any mystic markings nor special communings by special people. Limbs of trees rub themselves hot on dry days and make flame. The hot sun shining on the mica in the rocks set fire to the tiny mosses that are dried there. And so without human agency the fires come that are necessary to make our Australian seeds burst into the life of a new and growing plant.

The black people knew this, and they were well aware that the seeds must be burnt and so this knowledge gave rise to the legend written here.

WHY LEAVES FALL

The natives of the Urana district in Riverina had a little story about falling leaves.

No doubt other tribes had a legend about the same thing, for in most places there were legends about nearly all natural phenomena.

That those who were accustomed to the deep leaf-carpets of the coastal jungle, the masses of fallen leaves in the Dorrigo, of the gullies of the Liverpool Range, in the Hunter River Valley, the tract of sub-tropical bush under the Illawarra Range, in the back country of Gippsland, and on the south-western corner of West Australia, must have attributed the falling of the leaves to some obscure agency-magical and fearful and at the command of the doctors or the priests-goes, I say, without question.

The flora of the Urana district is as different from that of the other districts named as it well can be. In summer-the roasting, scorching summer-there is little but wilted grass and pathetic looking gums. The Murray Pines (Callitris) give a deep green relief to the depressing balance, and even they seem to cluster together for mutual protection. The quartz ridges produce a few miserable hakeas; the sandhills have a few rushes such as the dianella and the Juncus paucilorus if there happens to be a leakage or a soakage, and some stunted banksias and occasionally a zamia of some sort and perhaps a Richea and a little colonema giving out its strong lemon-like scent when broken; but of rich trees or matured shrubs or pretty flowers there are almost none.

In winter and spring this country is different. The rains of the cold season, if at all copious, make it possible for a wealth of grasses to grow, and happy are the horses and cattle and the sheep of the people out there who have broad acres. The Murray pines are aglow then, and the gums are fresh, and the few clusters of leaves on the stark branches rejoice with the people.

It is there that there is the story of the falling leaves. Why it should be there is a puzzle.

A great ancestor was named Wingaree. He is, so the aborigines I am now writing about say, the ancestor of brown snakes, goannas, water-fowl and all flying insects, and of those human beings whose totems are the mentioned creatures.

Where Wingaree lived there was a depression that was a lake in rainy times, and it was filled with wild fowl and many snakes and goannas by this Wingaree. The ancient gum-stumps that stood all worn and broken are weird in the extreme, and Wingaree still can be seen in some of them, and comes out when the water rises and fills the hollow. This is at the time of heavy rains.

During the rain great numbers of insects-gnats and termites and others-may be seen flying from them. When dry the lake was a rough mass of grey mud, and often duck eggs might be found sticking in it, the water evaporating before the eggs hatched. All round the depression and stretching as far as the eye could reach, the flat country is just as I have described, and when the haze danced and the mirage formed and rolled, it was an unreal and magic land.

There had been a long dry period. Wingaree, away back in the times of the beginnings of the worlds, lived in a tree that grew where the lake now is. He bad many children like himself, but he also had others that were not like him. The water-fowl and the huge goannas and the brown snakes and the insects were different. Black snakes were the children of his first wife, who had been married before.

Now there was much water in another lagoon not far from Wingaree's tree, and somehow a hole had come in the ground and the water had all gone down in it and had left the place dry. No rain came to fill it up again and Wingaree was as thirsty as everything else. His children left him. The waterfowl flew away to a far distant river, the goannas went underground to search for the water that used to be in the other lake, and the snakes crawled further still to a very big lake that always had water in it.

Wingaree was, however, very clever, and he believed that he could make rain. But he was afraid to put his powers to the test, for if he made any mistake the rain would be bad water or it would be too much and even he might be drowned.

So he at last decided to go where the rain came from and search out the spirit that was there; and one hot night when the moon was full and the air was scorched and the ground was baked and the grass was all burnt off and the trees were withered, he decided that he could go up into the sky.

A long cloud lay on the horizon, and Wingaree imagined that he could hide behind it and watch until the rain spirit came into view, and then he could step out and show his great respect and ask just how to make some rain for himself.

Wingaree left his tree and soared up into the sky and reached the place behind the cloud. There he sat watching until the rain spirit appeared.

It was too angry to speak. Wingaree tried all the ways that he knew to please and to persuade the spirit to tell him what to do. But it was all in vain.

However, the rain spirit stamped in his anger and that stamping so shook the cloud that it became rain, and the noise of the tramping travelled through the world, and a fire flew from his heels and shot down to the earth. Gradually then the cloud melted until there was none of it left, and Wingaree had no protection, and on one of the streaks of fire he came back down to his tree.

The great storm lasted for many days. The rain changed to hail and there was so much of that, that the place where stood the tree in which Wingaree lived was all filled up and he had to come out into the storm. The ground all around this tree was a thick mass of hail and it piled up until Wingaree was obliged to climb into the highest branches.

Then the storm ceased.

The snake children were safe. Many of the goanna children were drowned, but some came up out of the holes and they climbed the tree.

The water fowl had to fly in the air amid the rain and the hail because the lake to which they went became a raging sea, for the wind blew there. But when the storm ceased and the sun came out again the hail melted, and that which lay all about the tree became a water hole.

Wingaree came down into the water. As soon as he touched it the hail began to fall again. The sun was blotted out by a great cloud, and soon there was just as much hail as before. It splashed into the new lake and it piled up against the tree and it made the whole country a white mass.

Wingaree was unable to get any shelter. Water fowl still flew in the air, snakes still remained safe as before, but many goannas climbed the tree and clung to the trunk in such a mass that there was no room for Wingaree. He was their ancestor and he could not take their place nor could he destroy them while they did nothing that was against the rules.

Then one of the birds came to him. It had the white down on its breast that men get when they are about to worship, and priests get when they are going to perform any sacred rite. It was a special bird, and long afterwards the natives were very happy when they found out which one it was and they could get the soft, white down with which to decorate their bodies and thus please the ancestor who got so much good from the same bird.

It was the brolga.

The brolga made many bows and much obeisance before Wingaree. It stepped forward and then back. It swung round with its wings just a little open, and bowed again. It bent its long neck into a graceful bow and it lifted its feet one after the other in perfect time and almost in tune.

Eventually Wingaree was obliged to notice so graceful and respectful a creature, especially as he had brought it into being in the days long before those when all this that I am telling happened.

The brolga gave Wingaree some advice. It was that he must divide himself up into very many parts and each part must be able to fly. That, Wingaree did, and that is how it is that he is the ancestor of all flying insects. He was, however, as badly off as before, for the hail was still falling and much of him was being destroyed by it. He asked the brolga what he should do next.

Even while he asked there were very many insects being driven down to the ground and into the water. If that went on for long there would be nothing of him left, and all his children would be without an ancestor. Therefore the brolga called to all the water birds and they heard the call. They came flying in a great mass just as they do now in that part of the country when the rains come. The insects that were formed out of Wingaree spread all over the country and were still being beaten to death. So the brolgas set the other birds to biting the leaves of all the trees, especially the gums, and nipping them at their petioles, and they fell. Insects had taken refuge under the leaves, and as they fell those, parts of Wingaree were carried down and to safety. Hail might strike the leaves but the insect was still safe. And so, if one searched, there might be found an insect beneath every fallen leaf. The fowl had done their work in full, and since that time they did not go into trees, but the custom has been passed on to other birds.

Insects themselves, before they have wings, provide for their safety in their winged life by doing it. Then when they fly and the rain comes, they crawl under the fallen leaves.

And one of the strange things about this tale of the aborigine is that it is in such great part perfectly true.

Myriads of flying insects do come out of old stumps just before rain begins to fall and during the downpour, and it is also true that under all fallen leaves in the outback part of this country insects hide. They may be seen under each fallen leaf, having no doubt gone there to escape the terrific heat.

82

AT LOW TIDE

This is a story of, in part, the coming of white men to Australia.

Whether it is wholly true or not does not, perhaps, matter much.

It is true this far-that since the earliest times the aborigines did believe that a black man was taken by a great white spirit and he became the ancestor of the great white race. It was thought that this black man was so favoured by the god that he took him to his own realm, and that occasionally, at times remote from one another, some aborigine nearly as much favoured, was allowed to penetrate after death into the country of this white race and become white like the ones there, and then come back for a time to his people.

So we have many accounts of white people being taken to the hearts of the blacks just because they thought that perhaps those whites were the favoured blacks who came back.

Often a sear on the white man was the recognised mark; sometimes it was a peculiarity of hair; sometimes an uncommon walk, and sometimes there was some likeness in facial features. The blacks were all very quick to notice such things.

There are many stories of kindnesses done by the blacks at times when the white was powerless, and it is a fact that the traits of human character that make for benevolence and charity were pronounced in the autochonous inhabitants of this country.

All over Australia men and women watched for the return of the man who was taken to be the ancestor of a white race. On the great plains the vantage points were trees, but if there were an outstanding rocky eminence periodical pilgrimages were made to it. On the highlands the place was always a cool gully with moss and fern-grown sides, while on the coast it was always the highest of a line of sand-dunes or the top of a rock-bound promontory.

That white morning away back in the thousands of years ago that brought Allambee from his gunyah (he was called Allambee because he was slow in his movements), blinking at the sun that was just crawling up from beyond the edge of the sea, was just the same as the many white mornings that brought me out of my tent to look at the same sun steadily rising from beyond the horizon down on the New South Wales Coast, somewhere in the mists of my past.

But in Allambee's days there were different things everywhere. Whether of the animal world or the plant world or of the spirit world the aborigines were not clear, and from what they said, I believe that it was of the spirit world, for their belief in magic from above nature, and the supernatural in all things, was pathetically great.

The sky became brilliant. The sea was whitey-grey with specks of flashing silver coming from the sun to a wide mark just behind the breakers. These specks danced like shaking beads.

Away to the north the sea was calm and flat and still and light blue; away to the south it was just as calm and flat but a little bluer. The horizon was level and clear and sharp. The breakers were very lazy. They just reared up and broke in white foam and fell and came on and in. When they reached the beach they slipped in lines of tiny foam and turned and faded out. The beach was yellow and massed with shells and dry cuttlefish and a few old water-smoothed logs lay about on the sand. An irregular line of mesembryanthemum and marram-covered dunes stood then, and Xerotes rush with the pebbly and spikey flowers forbade unwary trampling. Big old gnarled Banksia serrata leaned over bowing to the sea, and the underscrub was leptospermum and bracken fern with a tangle of hibbertia and smilax and hardenbergias.

It was a clear patch that sloped to a wide rushy lagoon, and back of it all the flat-sided and sheer and dense-clad range.

Now, of this beauty all is gone but the sea and the sky, for white man is the despoiler of nature. The range is made bare. The lagoon is dried up. The banksias and the ferns and the bushes are all gone. The sand dunes are all torn away, and the shells are trampled and broken. The dust of civilisation and the dirt of coal mines and the dazing noise of industry-the, after all, useless industry-of white man, vilify the air.

When white men came the land was as Allambee saw it and as it had been for the ages. Whatever difference occurred was the difference of evolution, not of revolution. A flat patch of rock to the southwards that was edged with green mosses and sprays of seaweed caught the breakers and the mosses were sparkled and the seaweed swung with the water as it receded. When the tide was low and the waves just murmured and the seagulls swept the surface with their sharp wings there was a wide, low slope of beach.

Allambee walked amongst the sleeping people and stood on the sand dunes.

He saw a strange sight. A white man sat on the sea over against the flat patch of rock. He was very big.

He had flowing hair and a big mass of beard and his eyes could be seen even at a great distance. And in his hand he held a long spear.

Allambee had never seen such a spear before. He had never seen anything like this sight, for the man was huge and bright and white, and all about and belonging to this apparition was the same-huge and bright and white.

At first he was very frightened.

The sun came high up and the sparkling flashes became less and less and the white morning became blue and a little breeze sprang up in the north-east and came on in little pulses across the sea and stirred the leaves of the banksias.

The people moved and dogs stretched themselves and yawned.

Allambee forgot his fears and determined to go across to the rocks to see the big man who sat on the sea. He wanted to talk to him. The great stranger said that he had come to choose a good man to go with him to the place from whence he had come, for a king was wanted there to become an ancestor and to cause a race of people to come to inhabit the land and make it grow the beautiful things that were on other parts of the coast, especially that part which we call Illawarra. He asked Allambee if he would go, and though Allambee thought of his wife and his children and his people, he thought, too, that it would be fine to be a king, and what is so much better, an ancestor, so he consented to go. But he must return to the camp and have just one last look at those whom he really loved. He found his wife and his little brown baby on the sand dunes just where he had stood when he saw the big man out on the water. Others of the family group by this time were astir, and were either preparing food and weapons, or were trying to decide where they would hunt during the day. Many women were seated at fires, and watching to see the round stones become heated enough to use for baking meat and fish. Others were idly jabbing their digging sticks into the grass. The rest were either patting the dogs or just standing awaiting orders. Children were playing about-some in the lagoon and some on the sandy patches or amongst the green grass.

Some men were busy extracting the tough sinews from wallabies' legs to use as tying-string and binding their stone axes in the handles. Others were applying themselves to the cooking and the fashioning of weapons, as I have written.

None had gone to the beach. Only Allambee's wife had reached the sand-dunes, and there she sat awaiting her husband.

When he came he told her what had happened. She looked across to the rocks but she could see no man at all. She grew very much afraid, for she thought that if Allambee had seen any such thing he must be what the Scotch call "fey." So she said nothing, and taking her child close to her she rose simply, but with much trepidation and inward weakness, and went back to the camp.

Allambee followed.

All the people could see that something had occurred to Allambee, and the wife whispered that it was magical and no one spoke to him. They were afraid that he perhaps possessed magic power and that he might use it to their detriment or at least disadvantage.

So Allambee silently passed out from the people and going down to the rocks he waded into the water. Many of the family group went as far as the dunes and from there they watched. The principal watcher was his wife.

During many days that followed she went out there, and though other women tried to comfort her she would not be comforted. Her husband was not dead, therefore she did not wear the white clay that was usual, and that, being a dress of some sort, was, even in their distress because of the loss of a husband, a source of satisfaction. She did her work. She entered into the preparing of the food just as before. She tended her children. When the women went to the rocks either to the north or to the south to assist in the catching of crustaceans or the spearing of swimming fish or the trapping of eels, she went too. She made ropes of fur and bags of rushes and sea-grass, and she watched the black under her baby's skin gradually spreading over his little body, but in it all-during all her days, and while she was awake at night, she waited and longed for her husband.

She believed that one day he would come back and she would know him.

Then came the time when the king ordered the people to go to another part of the coast. While they were wending their way along the beach they came to a place where a creek spread itself out on the sand, and only a narrow bar separated it from the water of the sea.

Allambee's wife was the first to essay to pass along the bar. It was of sodden sand, and underneath that there was much soft and rotted weed. She sank. The sand was a patch of treacherous quicksand. Allambee's little boy was left without either father or mother. He was cared for by some of his relatives, for all those

86

people whom Allambee, by the rules of his race, might have married were considered as much mother as the real mother, and Allambee's brothers as well as those brothers of the women he could have taken to wife were uncles, so no orphan could ever be without relatives. When he grew up he became a priest and he thought that his father was taken by a spirit for some great work and that his mother had joined him. This belief was shared by the people and Allambee's son was looked upon with more awe than reverence. He was under instruction for many months but the day came when he was accredited, and after that his ministrations were accepted and he grew to be of great importance. The people had moved back and forth many times. He knew all the story of his father, and every time that the camp was back near those flat rocks he spent many mornings on the sand-dunes gazing out to sea and hoping to find his father coming back with the great white spirit with whom he had gone away.

When again the tide was full and the rocks were covered and the breakers dashed against the cliffs and the beach was under water he did not bother to look. If the storm blew and the rain fell, and the wind lashed the leaves of the banksias and twirled the bushes and the streamers of marram that grew on the sandhills he thought it was no time to watch, for then the sea was very rough and no one, not even a spirit, could walk on it.

His day at last passed away and he went out into the beyond and his people buried him in the sand. All the rest of the people who died were buried in the shallow graves further up the beach, and after a time their bones were taken up and scattered, but a member of the immediate family took an arm bone or a shin bone (a radius or a tibia) and carried it for luck until it became uninteresting or a nuisance, when it was thrown away.

But a bone of a priest was never taken.

Each successive priest in his day watched on the sand-dunes.

Then came a day just like that day on which the great spirit man appeared. The sun came up out of the sea in a white sky as before and the sparkling spots danced and spread on the water and the waves were weary.

A priest stood on the sand-dunes. Away out on the ocean the great white thing appeared. It rolled with the water.

The priest ran to the slumbering people and soon the sand-dunes were lined with men and women and children who watched the unknown thing out on the sea.

The tide went out. They fully expected it to turn and come in, and to see Allambee with it. The story of him was as fresh in the knowledge of the tribe as if the happening of his going was one of only the day before. The priests, one after the other, kept the story green.

There was not much work done that day. And all the conversation was about Allambee and the expected coming. The white thing was the first of many that came, and it was seen that white men came from them and sometimes white women were with the men.

These men and women were of the race that Allambee went to be the ancestor of, and to this race belong all men who go out black and return white.

THE BUBBLING SPRING

Away on the South Coast of South Australia there is a very interesting natural spring. It emerges from between two limestone rocks. In very wet times the flow is much less than during a period shortly before rain comes. Especially is this so when a drought is on the point of breaking. The surrounding district is very swampy, and great shallow reedy lakes stretch out over the land. There is the haunt of millions of wild fowl-ducks, cranes, spoonbills, herons, bustards, pipers, and swan, with an occasional pair of pelicans, and floating overhead the great lazy sea-eagle and many hawks.

The water teems with eels.

Just over the long lines of sand dunes at the back of the broad beach the flat sea sails leisurely in, coming on in small breakers which curl and foam and climb over receding ones. Far out on the level horizon floats a dark haze. Seldom is a boat of any sort seen.

Along the beach on the right or westward is a headland nearly out of sight, and to the left, looming above the water, is another.

This was the home of thousands of aborigines of the Boonadick Tribe. Inland, over the rushes of the lakes and the patches of tea-tree and stunted box, can be discerned the blue top of Mount Gambier. Mount Schanck is nearer, but it is not more than 700 feet high, and cannot be seen from the spring. The immediate surroundings of the spring are densely scrubbed. Banksias, melaleuca, leptospermum make a thick bush, and eucalypt-like mallee, with their twisted stems and tangled branches, shut out the glare of the sun. The spring itself is bubbling away day and night, week after week, year after year, century after century.

There are many springs. The whole coastline gives evidence of a leaking away of the great subterranean waters that ever flow from the thousands of miles inland towards the Great Southern Ocean.

The water is as clear as crystal.

Sandy bottoms, white and shelly, are as plainly seen as if the surfaces of the waterholes were just a sheet of beautiful glass. There is a faint greenish tinge owing to the presence of magnesia and gypsum. From Central Australia this artesian flow percolates through hard sponged cells; it falls into abysmal underground chasms; it runs swiftly down undulating tunnels that are deep down; it slides in subterranean tubes; it lies in places still as age-long death, though there must be current somewhere in it, for at last it emerges somewhere on the coast and joins the sea on the south-east.

The spring we are writing about is called the Bubbling Spring.

It does not "emerge." It gushes and gushes upwards. Many others gush, but none so interestingly as this.

To the Boonadicks the spot was tabu.

No Boonadick tribesman would go near it. Though the water gushes up, it does so in a fashion that has to be seen to be believed. There is no word that properly portrays the manner of the gushing. It assumes a wonderful shape. It swells out cask-like and then gradually becomes narrower until the highest level is reached, when it rolls over the edges and slithers downward over itself, making a form like a cask, and a cask of sparkling, greenish, undulating globules that remind one of the gems that are said to ornament a Buddhist temple, or that are decking the Madonna bust in the Church of the Holy Sepulchre at Jerusalem.

The aborigines would not look at it. They would sit just outside the dense patch of scrub with their backs to it and listen, and even chant a strange dirge; in keeping with its tone, but they would not push through the bushes and brambles and look at it.

They bad their legend, a weird tale, and no one knew whence it came nor when. It is the agonised breathing and struggling of a woman.

Great seals, beautiful and sleek, often came out of the sea and lay on the sands, especially during moonlight nights.

There was a time when the Bubbling Spring was not tabu.

Indeed, the water of its pool was medicated, and blacks who suffered aches and pains-probably rheumatism, used to drink there, and would allow the tumbling water to dash upon the affected part.

Now the Krubi of this tribe was a wayward child. Her mother knew that the girl's beauty was such that when the old Krubi died there would be no one to dispute that the place of a Krubi would be the place of her daughter, and it is probable that she was duly spoilt. Though the actual mother did not have a great deal to do with the rearing of children after a certain age, still she could make her presence felt, and this one did to the detriment of the little one.

When she should be near in order to do the work that should be her lot, she was mostly away by herself seeking her own amusement, and in all matters fending for herself. Once she was away four days, and when she returned, though she was beaten she refused to tell where she had been and what she had done. She it was who discovered that far out on the rocks there was another Bubbling Spring. It was nearly always under water. The sea water covered it at most high tides, but when it was very calm the bubbling could be seen. Occasionally a little crustacean would be caught in its upward flow, and he would come up like a shot, clawing, clawing, and sometimes twisting and turning until he was nearly to the top, when the force would be spent, and he would flounder and float and sink down away to one side of the bubbling.

He had had a lesson. He now knew of the strange thing, and for the rest of his life of a thousand years he avoided that strange stir and was never again caught in its fresh water.

For him that was the trouble. The water was fresh and he felt choked. There was nothing in it that was in the salt water, and that was life to him.

The young Krubi had seen all this before she told anyone else, and for a time the under-water spring was unknown. Then when she apprised the rest of the fact, it became something of surpassing interest, and little sea animals were captured and confined in grass nets and lowered into it and watched until death put an end to their sufferings.

One beautiful moonlight night Krubi was minded to wander off. Most of her people were asleep. Only a few prowlers, perhaps, with a disposition much like her own, were astir. They heard the quacking of the wild ducks and watched the bobbing floats of their fishing nets-bobbing that told of a plentiful haul of rush-meshed fish. Krubi avoided them, and gaining the beach she hastened along in the shadows of the sand-dunes towards the long low point away in the east. After walking for some time she espied a figure half-way up the sand and many yards from the fine light line of slowly swirling foam. She stood still for a moment, and then cautiously approached. The figure lay apparently asleep, for the girl went close enough to touch it. It was like a long, sleek, legless kangaroo. Its dark fur lay close, and glistened. Its sweeping lines, graceful and clear from its head over its shoulders and tapering to its flat tail, were perfect examples of the delineator's art. Its huge fore flappers were pressed into the sand, and though its broad head and whiskered snout stood up somewhat, it was undoubtedly asleep. It seemed to be black, but its colour was brown-a beautiful dark and rich brown.

Krubi recognised it to be the animal we call a seal. She knew that it lived on fish, and she knew that a small store of fish was placed under a vine not far away from the Bubbling Spring. So she hastened noiselessly back and gathered it up.

The seal still lay asleep, and even when Krubi stooped and placed the fish within its reach it did not stir until the fish-smell, drawn into its nostrils, awakened the desire to eat, and then it sniffed and awoke.

Krubi held a fish up to its mouth and it ate. She pushed the heap a little closer, and the desire of the seal to hurry off was overcome by its wish for food. And Krubi was able to pat it gently, and as it ate it looked at her with an expression that only a big seal has. There was wondrous intelligence shown in its eyes, and wondrous appeal in the poise of its head. Krubi was captivated, and when the seal was finished and awkwardly ambled on its flappers round and back to the water for the purpose of diving and playing, Krubi went out knee-deep in the tumbling waves and watched. Sometimes the seal came gambolling around her, brushing her legs with its sleek, slippery body, and playfully snorting as if asking for more fish. Krubi had no more, and wending her way slowly back, she noiselessly crept in amongst her sleeping people and went into the Land of Sleep with them.

The next night she sought the seal again. Night after night she watched, but it did not reappear.

Krubi always saved a little of the catch of fish that she was expected to cook, and at last one other clear moonlight night the seal was again on the beach. With it was another, even bigger. Krubi ran swiftly down the sands, throwing the meal of fish before her. The moon and the stars gave all the light that was necessary, and Krubi had no hesitation in running right up to the animals, and they had no fear. The first that came even flapped up to her and ate rapidly and ravenously. The mate was not so forward nor so friendly. He blared and he showed great sharp teeth.

She did not care for the newcomer. She gave all the fish. She would much rather her old friend had come alone. When the meal was finished the new one coaxed the other away, and she felt disappointed and angry. Then, to make matters worse, the loud blaring of the seal had been heard, and Krubi saw that several of the men of her people were hastening along the beach and others were lining the top of the sand-dunes with poised spears.

92

She sped past them and home.

Next day there was quite a noise about it, and Krubi's mother and her aunts scolded and the chief gave orders to them that Krubi was to be kept more under surveillance, and a couple of jealous women were set to watch her. So for many days and nights Krubi could not search the sands for the seal. She somehow missed it too, and she only waited until the vigilance was less by the spiers growing weary. Then she slipped away in the night again. Both seals were on the beach. She went down with a bag of fish. Both animals besieged her.

Suddenly a spear came swishing through the moonlight air and her pet was transfixed by it. The strange one was more fortunate. He turned and in his best fashion galloped into the sea. Fortunately for him the bottom shelved at the point and the water was fairly deep; therefore he was safe. There he could evade any spear. His hearing was so acute, his eyesight so keen and his movements in the water so quick that not only did he know when a spear was coming, but he could be so swift in his turning and his diving that he could not be hit.

And Krubi?

She was hit. A spear drove through her thigh. Because of the pain she rushed after the seal, and, becoming faint, she fell. Then a strange thing took place. The seal sped to her rescue. He dived so that he could get below Krubi and instinctively she dashed her arms about him and he bore her off. The men were much afraid. They hastened back and they awoke the chief. The whole tribe turned out and they waited on the sand-dunes or patrolled the beach in the hope of catching a sight of Krubi.

No one touched the stricken seal. It lay there until the tide grew bigger and it rolled out into deep water.

In the morning Krubi was seen. She was near the spring that swelled and spurted out amongst the rocks and under the sea. Plainly she was caught in it. Her mother scolded the men, saying that they were cowards and should brave anything to bring her in. The man who hurled the spear that struck her was clubbed to death. The chief ordered the flagellation and he was borne unconscious to the camp to recover if the spirit willed. The spirit must have decreed otherwise for he died.

After that two young men waded out into the sea. The tide was flowing and every minute the water was pouring deeper.

Of a sudden then the sky grew black. A great shaking took possession of the whole world. Hot ashes and hot stones rained down. The blue mount that lay away inland was coughing up fire and the earth all about rocked and was horribly shaken. For a moment the sea swirled backwards, and the rocks opened. Krubi disappeared, and the rescuers were carried out to be seen no more. The earthquake (for that it was, though there are those who declare that the blacks have no knowledge of any such happening) was something of only a moment.

Years later it was discovered that the tops of the distant mountains had fallen in, and the same clear, greenish-blue water that was in the swamps and in the Bubbling Spring filled the great holes, and it is there till this day.

But what of Krubi?

The great seals were spirits in that form. By an underground passage she had been taken inland. Once she was seen in the lakes of Mount Gambier. Afterwards she was heard in the waters of the swamps. Now she is beneath the Bubbling Spring. Any night she may be seen. The spot where she is trying to make her way up and out is the spring, and the noise of it is her breathing and her gurgling and her spluttering.

It is the Bubbling Spring.

The apparently dead seal disappeared, and sometimes on moonlight nights it too may be seen lying on the beach half way between the dunes and the tide.

THE SALT LAKES

The power that the aborigines possessed of bringing about their own deaths by an effort of will is generally looked upon by white people as one peculiar to what are mostly termed "Native Races." Just what is meant by "native races" is hard to define. But it seems to embrace those peoples of colour whose social status is looked upon as being less or on a lower plane than that of ours, and not on the level of brown people. Certain it is that our autocthonous predecessors in occupany of Australia had it and exercised it. No one of them had to jump over a Gap or sever a windpipe. Nor yet take a dose of poison. All he had to do was "go bush," hidden from all, and bring his spirit from his body by compelling it to come. The operation was accompanied by great sullenness and determined, self-engendered, depression.

In the same category, it is considered, is "Boning." Provided a person knew what marks to make in clay on the face, and what incantations to indulge in, he could kill by pointing a bone. Circumstances and surroundings had to be propitious. It had to be done in secret. When the envious mother decided to rid herself of the beautiful Krubi, as told in the story, "How the Waratah got its Honey," she prepared a bone and awaited the chance, as you have read. Had there been no interference and the plan had not miscarried in any particular, Krubi would have died.

There is the tale of the very tall man who was feared by his tribe simply because of his unusual height. If my conjecture be right, based as it is upon the description brought down by a third generation and the last a white, then this man of unheard-of growth must have been fully eight feet high. His father, said to have been thirteen stone weight, reached but to his waist. He wielded more power than the chief, and quite as much as the medicine man.

He was a "boner." There had been several mysterious deaths, and a polished bone was one of the secret possessions of the tall man. Several men had seen it. He took a violent dislike to the chief

95

because he had been instructed to prepare himself for participation in a corroboree, and he did not like the part he was to play. He, because of his height, was considered to be the best to show the young men how to climb a tree. He had to stride just as if he were climbing a winding stair, He had to portray just how to hold the trunk, just how to place the big toe in the bark, or just how to cut the notch in the side if the bark were not thick nor rough enough.

He failed to appear. Drums made by digging small round holes and stretching skins across them and pegging them down were fashioned and beaten. This always signified that someone was neglecting a duty.

The tall blackfellow took no notice. He remained just out of sight, and the corroboree had to proceed without him.

This could not happen many times. All the tribe talked of it. The chief knew that either he or the challenger had to go, and he decided that he would meet the defiance with cunning.

He ordered a war. Some time before river blacks had sent an insult in the shape of the chief totem mark of this tribe wrapped in feathers and tied to a spear, and this was thrown to an old woman. There was no disgrace in ignoring it, and that was done. But now he wanted an excuse to kill the boner and he made up his mind to fight the river blacks and if the boner was not killed at it he would be on the way back. The boner knew all that was passing in the chief's mind, and he laid plans too. He put a beautiful polish on his bone and determined that if he once saw the chief alone he would finish him with it, even if he were a chief.

To try his power with the bone he called his wife to him, and leading her out of sight of the rest he pointed the bone in her face. The unfortunate woman was seized with an ague and she did as all others did under like circumstances. She walked away through the ferns, through the scrub of myrtle and vines that made dense the bank of the creek, and then, crawling under there where it was hollowed and hidden by a mass of old dark roots and a fallen log, she lay down and died. Her tracks were followed by her sister, and her bones must be lying there still, for no one who died of boning was ever buried. They were left just where and as they lay.

So the bone was good.

A corroboree was held, and at it the young men who were not yet taught the arts of war were shown all about it. At that time the tall man was a teacher and he went to it as such because he thought he might get a chance to carry out what was in his mind.

The day of war dawned. Shields had been fashioned, spear-heads

96

were tested, and nullahs were swung to try their weight. A move was made up over the hill and into the mosses of the gully at the head of a creek that fell away to a flat and then rushed over boulders and amongst stones to where it joined a river. It was night before the river blacks were sighted. They were not unprepared. They had plenty of weapons and their women had for some days been hiding away on the timbered slope of another hill.

With fierce yells the bush blacks came on. They formed a few lines, and when the most advanced one was held up they got into open order and the second one came through. It was quite an organised affray, but the bush blacks were beaten. The river men had prepared too well. Many of the others were taken prisoner and the boner was amongst them.

The chief escaped. He had lost most of his ablest men and he was very downhearted. He knew nothing of magic nor the craft of the spirit. He had never drawn the mystic lines of clay about his body, and his chief sorcerer, in the person of the boner, was in the camp of the enemy and probably, he thought, killed. For it was not the custom of the blacks to take prisoners.

The chief decided to redeem the boner if possible, and if he were really still alive. If he rescued him he would not be under his displeasure, surely, and the feud would be abandoned. So he caused several maidens to be taken over to the river, but this was not enough. The men who took them there returned with the message that more than half their land was to be given up, and the boner was to stay. All the rest were to go back, but the tall man could not. This was not, of course, what the chief desired, but he had no choice. He sent a present of about twenty wallabies, and he took the cloaks of about twenty women and sent them all over. He also sent a message saying that he wished to speak to the tall sorcerer alone for a few minutes, and after that the river people could have the coveted territory, and he and his tribe would trouble them no more.

All this was conveyed by means of a messenger and a message stick, and the river chief went in person to give the answer, though he pretended that he had not read the message. This deceit made the bush chief very angry, and the reception he accorded the other was far from friendly. He insisted that he must have the tall man returned to him, but it was firmly refused.

When the river chief returned he visited the boner in the gunyah that had been made for him, and asked why his chief was so anxious to have him back.

The boner produced the bone. The very sight of it struck terror into the heart of the river chief. He snatched it, and running down to the river he flung it in. Immediately a thin streak of coloured water was seen flowing from where the bone fell.

It was of a pinkish tinge, and it soon stretched on down the stream and the end of it was out of sight.

This river did not reach the sea. It was either lost in the flat country far on or it flowed into a lake.

Years afterwards two blacks from away there came up the river. Their people had lived for thousands of years around and about this lake. Nearly all their food they got from it, they said. But now it was changed. It had gone a strange pink colour, and the water was unfit to drink.

All wild fowl left it. The weeds with succulent roots died. Other growths took their place, but they were not fit to eat. Even the fish and the yabbies died, and so these young men determined to follow the river up to find the cause. They were provided with the proper message stick and they had the signs to any tribes whose territory they might pass through that they were on a very friendly mission.

They heard the story of the bone and they found that the river at the point where it had been thrown in was salt.

Ever since the lakes have been salty, and all salt lakes are fed from a river into which some sorcerer has thrown the bone with which he achieved the deaths of all he wished to secretly destroy, if he were a boner.

NOTE.—Some people who have been on most intimate terms with the blacks aver that "boning" is more than simply pointing. They say that the expression "to point" is the only one the natives had when they wished to convey something like "to shoot." They did not mean that the bone was only "pointed." They actually pierced. And first they charred the end of a green bone. This is said to produce prussic acid, and that, when inserted into a human being causes active and rapid blood poisoning.

Of this the writer heard nothing from, the blacks themselves, but as some of his information is from white men, perhaps he should take this as truth.

SHOOTING STARS

There was once a very great aboriginal king who lived somewhere in the belt of basalt country where the waratah does not grow. The hard rocks of this country have once been subjected to terrific heat. In fact, they are born of fire, and this the people knew very well. For a long time the king had been a very good king, doing all he could for the people over whom he ruled. He had all the prowess that a chief should have. His spear he could hurl furthest and straightest. His nullah struck hardest, and his boomerang always sailed in its twirling rings and pretty curves out further into the air and returned to sit poised and still twirling above the players and himself before striking the ground at his feet. His killing boomerang never failed to bring down game.

But when he was growing old he developed the whim to roam the bush alone. He lost the desire to remain the chief. All he did for the tribe was search out the best bits of fallen stone so that his artisans might grind them into tomahawk blades, axe heads, or spear points.

One day a thick mist fell amongst the rugged hills and he lost his way. He had travelled over the saddle between two rounded peaks, and descended into a ravine on the other side. He went on and ascended other peaks and went down into other gullies until he grew tired and then he essayed to return to the camp. But he was not sure that he had negotiated as many ridges and tramped through so many gullies, for they were all so much alike that it was very difficult for anyone to know one from another. When he realised that he was lost-had failed to remember in what direction he had come-he simply sat down to wait until the mist was clear away. But rain set in and he grew very cold. Then night fell, and as everything was wet he could not make a fire. He quite remembered the steep of the fall of the ground on the side of the first peak, and though it was still dark he walked as much to make himself warm as to find the way. He crossed over high ground and went into other deep places, and at last he felt that he was going down a steep

99

enough place to be where he had started to climb, and there he rested until the day broke. The mist was lightened and he could see that he was not at the place where he wished to be and where he was when the fog first shut out the scene. There the trees were the white-barked tea-tree and the underscrub was wire-grass and small rushes. But here were gums and wattles, and the undergrowth was Macrozamia and Chorizema and Wild Fuschia and Clematis and Sarsaparilla vine.

And it was much deeper. He knew all the plants that grew in his part of the country. He, of course, had his blackfellow names for them. The Acacia glaucescens, with its long yellow rolls of pollen he called "Karrawan," and the beautiful little Dillwynia ericifolia he called "Wannara"; the white-flowering Bloodwood he called "Mannen," and the pretty Wonga Vine he knew as "Telaaraweera," and so on.

What was he to do now? His hand had lost its cunning. His mind was not so alert. Unless he could find the tribe soon, he must die of cold and hunger. So he turned and endeavoured to go back. He climbed again the steep mountain-side and on top he was amongst many boulders, and the tussocked grasses and the burrawangs were such as he had never seen before.

He blundered on. In his anxiety he became uncertain of foot and often he faltered and almost fell. The rain came on again and the mist-the clouds that fell to earth-rested once more about him. He coo-eed, but no answering coo-ee came to him. Several days went by and it still rained and was still cold and misty, and it gave no promise of clearing. He had found roots in plenty but he lacked animal food, especially its fat, which was his most nourishing article of diet. He lived, though he grew weaker. At last he found a track. He knew it to be the well-beaten track of the brush wallaby, and he reckoned that if he waited patiently that night beside the path and hidden, he would intercept the animal, and meat and fat would be his. During the night the rain ceased, and a wind sprang up that shook the water from the leaves and blew away the clouds.

He hid beside the wallaby track and he had not long to wait.

Thud, thud, crash, crash, thud, thud-the wallaby was coming down from the ledges above to browse on the succulent grasses of the level and clear country.

The black man was patience itself. He grasped his nullah more firmly, and with one hand parting the leptospermums before him he decided just when to strike the blow.

It is strange that no white man can get a wild animal so. Wild things see him or smell him; besides, he cannot wait. The marsupial hopped unsuspectingly on, stopping every little while to nibble at some young shoots that overhung or infringed upon the track. Then, like lightning, the nullah sprang into being and it shot out straight to the wallaby's ear. He went down and his life went out with the trickle of blood that wandered slowly and brokenly down from the place where it had been struck. He had certainly made a feeble defence with his clawed feet, but before one reached his ear it wavered and quivered and fell.

Next day the man ate and was filled, and then he slept-a sounder sleep than he had had since he left his tribe. The wind that had been but a slight zephyr sprang into life. It grew stronger and stronger, and increased until it roared through the great gum-trees like a mighty torrent of water. The huge branches were tossed, and they swayed and crashed amongst one another and were twisted apart and fell. The small twigs snapped and were whirled about and strewed the ground like thick moss. The huge bark trunks leaned and strained and groaned and split and often cracked and thundered down. Giant masses of cloud swept overhead. A bird now and then essayed flight and was whirled and dashed to death. Wallabies and rats and dingoes grew afraid, and, leaping from the safety of their sheltered places, they sped off, bounding amongst the roaring trees and being twirled and blown and staggered in the awful gale.

The man slid down a crumbling bank into a bouldered creek. There was safety there unless the creek rose. If a tree fell it could not crush him; and trees did fall, but not one nor yet a broken limb caught him. They fell across the creek and rested on the boulders, and beneath it all he was not only safe, but warm.

Just as suddenly as the gale sprang up so it went, and as is usual it was followed by another great downpour of rain. He had to climb out of his shelter, and he found a hollowed stump which served, and with the remnant of the wallaby he felt that he could be comfortable until the storm ceased altogether. After two days the sun came out warm and the vapour steamed off the earth and sailed up through the tree-tops and into the sky from which it came. The blackfellow pushed on to a top, and shading his eyes with his hand, he peered away over the gum-trees, searching the lines of ridges as shown by the colouring of foliage, looking for smoke.

Ah! There was smoke! It was a long way off, but he would make towards it. He knew he would have to walk all day. Towards evening he ascended another hill-top and found no vantage point, so he

101

climbed a tree, and from there he descried the smoke again. It was not in the same place, therefore the tribe must be moving, and moving fast. He decided to camp there for the night, and be fresh to push on in the morning. He realised his old age, for each evening, for many evenings, he looked for the smoke and always it seemed as far off as ever. Several times he came across the fires. Once he disturbed the dogs that stayed behind to gather up the remnants of the food. There were often some dry roots or partially eaten meat or bones that had pickings lying about, and upon that scanty fare he did well enough. He made signal fires but they were unanswered.

The country changed. The basalt rocks-the sharp, brittle, ringing stone disappeared, and the ridges were ridges of sandstone. Vegetation was different, too, and there, just in front of him, was a plant and flower the like of which he had never seen before. It did not grow in his basalt region. He plucked it and smelt it and parted its pistils and found it to be full of rich moisture.

"Meewah," he whispered, meaning "sweet"! "Waratah," he said, meaning most beautiful!

Yet he now grew afraid. What tribe was he following? This was, he knew, far from his country, and he, perhaps, was only rushing or travelling into great danger and distress. So, gathering a bunch of this wonderful flower, he turned about and intended to try in another direction to reach his own tribe.

But he was too late. A couple of men of the travelling people had returned for something, and they espied him and called to him to stop. He did not quite know their language, but he sensed their intentions. He dropped the waratahs and faced them. All they did was to pick up the flowers, and by pointing, order him off.

They did not harm him.

In a few more days he saw other smoke and then he found his own people. He had a great tale to tell. Away in the direction which he showed, a wonderful flower grew. Its bush was beautiful, its form was unique, its colour was gorgeous and it had a sweet juice that he had sipped. It was "meewah" and "waratah"-sweet and beautiful.

A few of the daring ones agreed to go in search of it. Selecting the best of their weapons, and, with the old chief to guide them, they sallied out. It proved to be only about six days' march to the place where the wonderful flowers were growing. The country was an upheaval and outheaval of sandstone. The rocks were plainly thrown there by static pressure, and they were not caused by fire, but by successive layers of sand washed by running water. And the soil was scanty and poor and full of gravel. It was rich, however, in just what this pretty flower needed, and the roots of the stunted gums kept the soil friable and gave the underground stem of the waratah its proper food.

The party plucked many plants. They destroyed, too, for they did not understand its habits. They broke the stem from the brittle root and carried it away.

Shortly afterwards they went again. By this time the owners of the grounds had found traces of the marauders and they lay in wait. They made a great outcry. There was a great hurling of spears and some death cries. The fight was soon over. Not one of the trespassers ever returned to his people.

Now amongst them there was a great sorcerer. He knew more of the mystic signs and the daubing of pipeclay and the sending up of smoke through a hollow trunk than any other of his folk. Often he had saved the tribe. When food was scarce he could find it. When rain was needed he made it with his magic and his smoke magic. And now he was killed. His non-return and the continued absence of the chief were rightly interpreted. The chief's son was made chief with all due ceremony. A corroboree was held under the new chief and every lad who was anywhere near the fighting age was initiated and tried out. At this corroboree the young chief worked himself up into a state of great frenzy and this communicated itself to all those present. He grew passionate with no attempt to check himself. In this way he increased in daring and when he felt himself fit and had engendered sufficient boasting on the part of the young men, he gave the order to go to war. Their medicine man and their chief were to be avenged, or brought back if alive, though none believed them to be alive.

They were only three days following in the wake of their missing people when they found all the evidence of their fate. They went on. The waratahs were in bloom and they marvelled at the glorious sight. But they were bent on retaliation, and they wasted no time. The scouts of the rearguard of the tribe here were not slow to learn of their coming. They sighted the formidable spears and the huge bark shields. They sighted, too, the determined attitude of this band of fighting men. They reported to their chief, and orders for the women and children to go down into a walled-in gully with but one avenue of approach were given, and the women went down-all but two young ones who trembled for the safety of their lovers, and who ran the risk of defying the old women so that they could watch the battle.

The little band yelled and rushed upon their enemies and the spears flew. Those from the tribe fell harmlessly. The little band reserved theirs until they were only a few yards from the foremost of the opposing men, and then together, as one man, they hurled theirs. Every one found the intended billet. The great mob wavered and then turned and fled.

Then came a wonderful and inexplicable thing. It was a great bright light, burning blue, and travelling at an enormous rate. It came down out of heaven and no one knew who had caused it, but all believed that it must have been some sorcerer greater than any ever known. The earth trembled because of the speed of the visitation. The air was filled with hissing sound. The glare dazzled, and in a fraction of time the thing had struck the earth. The ground heaved and was rent. Stones went up, masses of earth flew, a terrific explosion roared. The noise of the burst was deafening, and it reverberated around and amongst the hills and through the bush until all the world was just a great full noise. The fighting men fell flat, and there they remained until the young women who had stayed to watch the battle came to them, for they were the first to recover their senses. They were full of consternation seeing no men standing up, but all lying as if killed, and each ran to her lover. There was really nothing wrong with the men. They were only stricken with a terror they had never before experienced. They looked up expecting to find, no one knows what, and seeing the girls their spent courage in some measure returned.

But what of the others? There was no trace. The terrible thing had wiped them right out, and of them there remained not a vestige.

And just beyond them the waratahs stood serenely, for not one was hurt. They were, and still are, quite immune from the effects of such fire.

That is why the blacks brought the waratah stems to the early blacksmiths. They thought that the sparks from the anvil were the same fire as that that came from the sky that day.

During the ensuing night more heavenly fires darted hither and thither. The frightened people grew somewhat accustomed to them and they watched them. They believed that the fires fell because the waratahs were being taken by those who had no right to them, and always the coming of a meteor or the shooting of stars was held to be a sign that the bright red blooms were being stolen.

There is quite another story of shooting stars that is told in those parts of Australia where the waratah is unknown. There they are said to be souls returning, and often men may be seen searching for them. Some even say that they have seen them and they show something that they say they got from them.

WHY THE PETIOLE OF THE WARATAH IS LONG

It was noticed by the aborigines that the leaf of a waratah has a long petiole, and the leaves of many other plants have a petiole that is very short. For instance, the waxy green leaves of the Diploglottis with its bunch of yellow berries, the Prostanthera lasianthos, the Chorizema, the Lilly-pilly (Eugenia Smithi) have but short petioles; while many of the eucalypts, the Honey flower (Lambertia formosa) as well as very many others have petioles like that of the waratah. None however is so long.

No one must imagine that such a thing of the bush could have escaped the notice of the aborigines. Many are the indications that our autocthonous predecessors saw a very great deal of the intimate habits of the flora and the fauna and the avifauna, and spoke freely of them, and attributed in their legendary many of these habitsmuch of the particular form and colour, and even habitat, to the influences of supernatural beings and occurrences.

Of the petiole of the waratah they said it is long because of a happening of seismic nature.

There was a camp one time on a volcanic field (presumably that of which Mount Wilson is the highest point) that was a scene of a weird and awesome happening. The tribe had been housed there for a long time, for the blacks of the Hunter River Valley had grown very strong, and were not afraid to penetrate into the territories of the Hawkesbury River people and the people of the flat of Hartley.

But the way to the Mount Wilson region was a difficult way. The Hawkesbury tribe and the Hartley tribe had joined forces and established the camp on the heights. The story, mentioning a fire from underground, is one of the few that show that the aborigines had a knowledge of time when Australia suffered from volcanic upheavals and earthquakes of volcanic origin.

There was game in plenty. Red rock wallabies were in millions, and many were the rugs made of their skins, and had they been trimmed with the red crests of the gang-gang cockatoo they would no doubt have equalled that wonderful cloak of the original Krubi.

Scouts had sighted blacks of the Hunter River tribe penetrating the gullies that led into the Grose, and of the Grose itself. Several corroborees were held to initiate the young men into the mysteries and methods of warfare. Every one was on the "qui vive" and tenterhooks. Watch was being kept both by day and by night. One young man, full of prowess, and eager to show his skill and resource to the maiden of his eye, had enwrapped himself in the skin of the wombat, and crouching on all fours had penetrated down, travelling only at night, to within a few yards of the outposts of the enemy. During the day he curled himself in a log or a hollow place between rocks, and many times he had been peered at and not been recognised. Then slowly creeping back he had brought tidings of the encroachments and strength of the marauders. But many weeks went by, and still no really hostile move was made by either party. The only wrong was the trespass.

At last the Mount Wilson people decided to drive the others away. They thought that by taking the initiative they would be the gainers because talkative men and women had twitted the rest, especially the young warriors, with idleness and cowardice. Down in a gully that had a flat area beside the creek a clearing was made, and stones were placed in position for the great and last corroboree before the engagement.

The day had been very hot and a dark mist had gathered toward evening. The whole mountain region seemed prepared for, or expectant of, something.

The blacks took no great interest in the coming corroboree. Only those who were over eager to fight seemed ready for the school. Yet the whole adult tribe repaired to the chosen spot.

When darkness fell the women seated themselves in the usual circle and were ready with their waddies to beat the earth in time and tune.

Then the world shook. The rumbling of an earthquake sped upon them and rolled beneath them and the hillside tumbled. The country rolled first one way and then another. The trees leaned with the rolling and righted when the earth righted.

There was nowhere to run. All eyes were turned towards the camping places, for there were the young people who could not attend a corroboree. But between them and the top of the hill an opening came and tongues of flame shot out. A few hot stones rolled down into the clearing, though no one was hurt. Then smoke arose and fire flared and the camp was seen to be ablaze. Cries and

106

lamentations filled the air. Then a youth named Camoola cried out for the man who had crept far in the wombat skin and knew everything. He must know, he said, where the fire came from, and how to put it out!

Now the blacks had for ages used the stem of the waratah to enwrap any hot thing they wished to handle. They said that it entirely prevented burns. In the earliest days of white occupancy of Australia they brought these stems to blacksmiths and told them that they could never be injured by fire from the anvils, which they took to be supernatural fire such as that seen in the heavens when there is a meteor travelling there, if they used them, and to please the natives the blacksmiths did use them and paid in those showy trifles that the natives valued, for them.

Seizing a couple of waratah stems, leaves and all, this young man sped out into the night. The rocking of the earth had ceased, but the fire burned on and the tongues of flame still leapt along the whole length of the great crack that came in the mountain-side.

Then Camoola, too, dashed off. He had plucked many waratah stems for he knew they would be needed. His wonderful hearing told him where Wombat-skin had gone. He reached him just as he was dropping down into a cave. The heavy dark mist had cleared all away. The stars now shone clearly. The camp was wiped out, and many injured people were writhing and wailing and could not be succored.

Holding the waratah stems out in front of them both Camoola and Wombat-skin dropped down into the cave. They cautiously went forward. They came to a bend, and rounding this they came in sight of the fire. It seemed to be coming up from a depth below, and it swept along the crack that passed here through the cave. If they could prevent it from coming up then the rest of their people could cross the crack at their point and reach the place where the camp had been.

Camoola ran back to the entrance where he had seen many waratahs. The bush was now afire at the entrance to the cave, and the waratahs could be plainly seen in its light. But Camoola could not climb out. He had dropped down without trouble, but there was no foothold whereby he might get out. He strained every muscle. He leapt high, but not by several inches could he reach another waratah. He went back to Wombat-skin. This brave young man was carefully wrapping himself up in his wombat skin, and sticking about it all the waratah stalks that he and the other had brought, for his intention was to lie across the hole and thus prevent the fire

107

from coming out. Only could Camoola stop him by catching his arms, and, being the stronger, he held him too tightly.

Camoola urged him to return to the mouth of the cave and to see if more waratah stems could be got before he essayed the dangerous task of lying across the fires. So they went back. Neither of them, nor the two together, could reach them. Then Camoola thought of the magic clay and he looked for it, and to his delight he found it. Hastily making the markings he had seen often enough on the priests, he invoked the aid of the spirits. He had yet to attend the school at which those were taught who were to be magicians, and therefore he did not fully understand the rites. He quite well knew that if he succeeded in obtaining aid he, being really uninitiated, would suffer for it.

Wombat-skin tried to jump again, but though the mystic signs were used he failed. It was now believed that an evil spirit stood near. Both men yelled to exorcise the evil of it. Both had heard the yell at the corroboree that they were not permitted to see, and knew what it meant and what it would do.

They jumped again and again. They grew strangely weak. They could jump no higher. Then the little stalk that joined the leaf to the stem grew. It became long quickly. The men could grasp them quite easily. They gathered a bunch. They covered themselves and one of them lay across the hole. The flames were stopped. The charm of the waratahs acted. They were not burned.

Outside the members of the tribe who would have joined in the corroboree shrieked with delight. They saw the flames cease. They too twined some stems of the waratah around themselves, and especially about their feet, so that the hot stones would not injure them, and they set out for the camp on the hill. They were weary before they reached it and saw how their folk were stricken.

Wombat-skin stayed with Camoola. He lay still in death. It is said that he touched a waratah stem while it was still being influenced by the hand of the spirit, and he, being uninitiated, could not bear the contact and he paid for it with his life. The waratah he touched was arrested in its growth, and the happening is perpetuated in those that are imperfect. They should be serrated and are smooth-edged. They should have the usual long petiole, but they have not.

Camoola was left in the cave, and many years afterwards-many centuries-his bones were found by the botanist Cayley.

Cayley penetrated the Blue Mountains to a spot where a great rock wall prevented his further exploration. Here he erected a cairn of stones, and the place is called now Cayley's Repulse.

Mount Wilson shows all the signs of volcanic eruption.

The trespassing blacks saw the fire and felt the quake, and they made all haste back to the Hunter Valley. The tribes that had amalgamated separated again and each buried their dead. No one dared to touch Camoola.

The clearing that was made for the corroboree is still to be seen at Mount Wilson. The great volcanic crack may also be seen at its foot and all agree that in the ages ago the happening described took place.

Mount Wilson and its neighbour, Mount Tomah, may be seen from any eminence of Sydney, and some say that the petioles of the waratah are longer there than anywhere else.

WHY THE WARATAH IS FIRM

The whole George's River tribe were camped on the flat between the bouldered cliffs that stand up high on each side of the stream. The weather had been very dry. Hot winds brought the yellow dust from the and regions of South and Central Australia and they wilted the vegetation of New South Wales and parched the people. One of those droughts, so well known to us, was withering the land. Though the happening took place many thousands of years ago, and though the story may have been altered in the telling by so many fathers right down the line, the story of the drought is the same as that we can tell of such a dry time.

The river had not been in flood for many moons, or, perhaps, years. Fish and eels were scarce. Only the big holes had them. Those holes are very deep, especially in that part of the river that has great flat rocks lying athwart it and stretching out on each side of the bed. Seventy feet is considered to be the depth at many places.

Most of the people were lolling in the shade. Only the hardiest stood motionless on the rock bottom with poised spear, while the hidden baiters gently scattered fine pith from the cabbage palm or chewed up seeds of the macrozamia, to attract the fish and bring them to the surface.

Warmeela, the son of the King, was the hardiest of all, and Krubi, his lubra, was never done warning him about the risks he took in war and in the hunting. Even now she stood under the myrtles, and with a waratah that she held in her hand she beckoned Warmeela to come to her.

Warmeela took no notice. Instead, he glanced to the west, for away over there great thunderclouds swelled slowly but surely up, and the faint zephyr that swung softly down the ravine ceased altogether. The hot air stood still. The only movement was the thrust spear as with a zip it pierced the water, and the quick kick of the impaled fish as he was suddenly lifted out and dropped into a crevice that prolonged his life for a little while, but in the water of which he soon struggled his last.

110

Then came the roll of thunder. The clouds blotted out the sun. A shade like the blackened haze of an eclipse spread over the river. One of the baiters went back to the myrtle scrub. Warmeela remained. Then the other went, and only Warmeela still stood by the hole. The tribe was moving back to a huge cave they knew of that had been formed by the rolling together some time long since, of several boulders. There was shelter for every man, woman, and child.

Warmeela's spear was poised. Like the cracks of millions of whips at the one time the first crash came and with it a frightful jagged fork of lightning. Warmeela was struck. His spear was hurled from his hand over the water, and stuck quivering many feet deep in a soft place on the opposite bank. There was a charred mark down its whole length, and the bone point was wrenched off. Warmeela lay prone amongst his struggling fish. A brother rushed to him and bore him back to the tribe.

Rain poured down. Roll after roll, crash after crash; thunder and lightning shook the hills. The wind came tearing through the giant gums and swirling amongst the shrubs.

Warmeela was unconscious of it all. He knew nothing of the consternation of his tribe. His old mother chafed his hands and the king gazed stupidly. Krubi, his pretty wife, held his head on her arm.

The storm rolled off again as quickly as it came, and then Warmeela opened his eyes. They were now useless. A print of a gumtree lay across his face, and the limbs were marked over his eyes. His sight was gone. A white streak appeared in his jet-black hair and one arm hung paralysed at his side. The next morning he tried to walk, and it was seen that he had a terrible limp.

Blind!

Now Warmeela was most fond of the honey of the waratah. The great Doryanthes excelsa produced much honey, but ants and gnats got that. Seldom did any aborigine regale himself with the juice of that flower, because he did not like the taste of ants nor the stings of flies. The waratah was different. Its honey, though less, is sweeter, and mostly there were no insects in the flower at all. But though it may seem strange to us, the bloom of the waratah was at that time very soft.

That was the statement of a broken-hearted native, whom the white called Griffiths, to the pioneer out Taralga way about sixty years ago. His real name was Coomerkudgkala.

Poor Warmeela. He had been so strong, so agile, so big hearted and so high-spirited. He now stumbled amidst the rocks. He would suffer none but Krubi to lead him. And often Krubi had to engage

111

herself with those things that women did, but always before she was half through the task, Warmeela called her. If she did not come at once he went off by himself.

The waratahs were blooming again, for a year had gone by, and Warmeela often put out his hand hoping to feel one.

He still hated to be handed anything. He wanted to feel and fetch and carry for himself.

Two flowers bothered him. The big yellow Podolepis acuminata and the flower of the native Musk (Olearia argophylla) often deceived him, and once some other flower poisoned him.

One day Krubi, his beautiful wife, came upon him when his heart was sad and he was ill and depressed. She asked plaintively the reason for his sadness. Warmeela felt for her hand and answered slowly, saying that he did not know one flower from another. He said he would drink of the honey of the waratah, but he could not find it. He too often mistook others for it.

Krubi promised that she would find a way so that Warmeela should always know the flower he wanted so much.

She led him to the place where the lightning had struck. She found a mark of it on the rock and she followed it knowing not why. Warmeela was willing to hold her hand and be led. The mark lay straight on over the flat rocks and the boulders, to the eroded bank. It showed on the bare root of a gumtree that it had split. Krubi looked up at the shape of the tree and she saw that it was the one printed on her husband's face. She sat beside the gum and there she was inspired. She spoke, and Warmeela did not understand the words. No one knows what she said. After a time she got up, and bidding Warmeela to wait, she sped over the rocks and logs until she found the beautiful red waratah. She returned with it and held it close to the crack in the gumtree. The soft pistils were drawn up and they stiffened. Krubi held the flower to Warmeela, and when he felt the difference he clasped his big hand over it. He clasped too hard. He bent the red pistils. In that moment a big red light lit the sky. A red ball descended, lighting up the firmament in such a way as to startle all who saw it. Some screamed and rushed about.

Not so Krubi nor Warmeela. They knew what no one else knew. The prayer of Krubi had been answered and thenceforth Warmeela would have no difficulty in distinguishing the flower he loved.

112

THE FIRST CRAYFISH

Perhaps no white man, hunter, or fisher, was so clever at catching any sort of game as the blacks, and perhaps no "native race," not even the red men of America, about whom we have read so much, who were so painstaking in their snaring, their stalking, their lying in ambush, so shrewd and stolid and picturesque, showed the patience, the cleverness, the agility, the keenness that were the universal attributes of our blackmen. Clever writers about the Reds of the West have told how they rode, and how they ambushed, and of their relentlessness, but not one story shows that they had the bushcraft the equal of that of the Australian aborigine.

This story deals with the catching of fish. No lines, no hooks-just rush nets and bare hands, and spearing, and the spearing was only done when the fish was big.

Of all the fishers of the Shoalhaven people none was so clever as a certain Krubi. She left it to other women to dig the yams. She caught fish.

The camp was a permanent one. Its location was somewhere near the site of the bridge of Nowra. High rocks sheltered it from the southerly winds, and a deep forest prevented the westerlies from reaching it.

Krubi caught fish with her hands. She used a bait of meat (too bad, by the way, for us to have handled), and this she hung between her own shapely black feet. When the fish were ravenously fighting for the food, Krubi simply drew her feet up and up. But this "simply" is just the requisite thing, and therein do we white people fail. True it is, though, that our superior knowledge and inventiveness have given to us means whereby we can catch as the blacks did not; though the very ease with which we may get big hauls is the undoing of our catching, for we caught to waste. Blacks never caught more than filled their immediate need.

Slowly but surely Krubi drew the bait. The movement was so uniform that not a tremor disturbed the meat, and not a ripple appeared on the water. Then Krubi's supple arm straightened. The hand entered the water wonderfully cleanly, and it was gently lowered with the long black fingers closed on a fish. There was no escape for it. Quick as a flash it was drawn up and the dexterous toss that landed it was the acme of cleverness.

The men of the tribe made bark boats. They carved a great ellipse of bark from the turpentines and from certain gums, and wrenched it free without a crack. Yet never did they ring a tree, for they knew that the bush of Australia was their living.

We are cutting our living out.

The blacks caught the ends of the piece of bark—two men to each end-and rapidly see-sawed it over a smoking fire. The best smoke was that made by throwing the branches of the Callitris calcarata on the fire. When the 'piece had been smoked sufficiently they placed a heavy log in the centre, the smooth side of the sheet being uppermost, and bent it to form the sides and the gunwale. Then the ends were easily drawn together and sewn with rawhide or sinews of the kangaroo. The tiny crack was caulked with rushes and mud, and as a last means of making the ends watertight they were smeared over with beeswax. Tingles and thwarts bound with rawhide were fixed, and the whole craft was constructed in less than three hours.

Krubi stood by one day watching the boatbuilders, and as she had become noted for her success at fishing she was allowed to show her interest in the work. Immediately the boat was launched she sprang lightly into it.

The other women of the tribe were aghast; never did they dare to enter a boat uninvited. But the men seemed pleased to allow Krubi to take advantage of the admiration so plainly bestowed upon her, and together they set off down the river in great glee.

Somewhere near its mouth there was a deep hole, and there the yabbies were unusually big. When this place was reached and the boat was beached the men set to work to fashion a net. Krubi remained in the craft and tried for yabbies. She had the usual piece of putrid meat, and breaking a part off she tied it to the end of a long stick. This she put into the water close to the big stones, and when it was bristling with clinging yabbies she drew them, clinging to the bait, right out and into the boat.

Catching yabbies was easy work. But in one haul there came up one bigger than all the rest. Amongst yabbies he was a giant. Krubi faltered when she picked him up, and a little spine on its head pricked her finger. The warm blood flowed upon the wet fish and it spread all over him.

This warm blood was a new and startling thing. Yabbies are not accustomed to anything as warm as human blood, and this one, startled as he was and being so big, jumped high in the air and landed with a splash back in the river. With great kicks he drove himself through the water, every now and then giving himself a mighty shake in an endeavour to throw off the warm liquid that was strange to him. On and on he went, down to the sea. The black men heard the splash and asked Krubi what had caused it.

Krubi excitedly told the story and showed her wounded finger.

Shortly after the net was set the people decided to pull further-to pull and sail on the current of the river right into the sea should the weather remain calm and the sea smooth.

They went round the point and into a sheltered cove, and there they hove to. Krubi was gazing over the side, when what did she espy but the big yabbie!

However, in a moment it had disappeared. She told about it, and many were the expectant glances and long looks that were sent overboard, but it did not again come into sight.

Many times afterwards fishermen of her tribe rowed round the spot, but it was not for some years that anyone again saw the curiosity. Krubi had grown middle-aged and had given up the pranks that she indulged in when she was young.

One day a son of hers caught a red yabbie. It was with intense delight that he hastened to the camp to show his mother the wonder.

She spat her disgust. It was not nearly big enough. It was red certainly, but it was far too small to be the one that had pricked her finger those long years ago. She said that there must he others and that this one came from them. She saw that a race of red yabbies, big and strong, was brought into being, and she knew that the first had been reddened with her warm blood.

115

THE CLINGING KOALA

There was but little of the habits of the indigenous fauna and avifauna of Australia that the aborigines did not well understand.

How many white people gave our native animals credit for the possession of the same senses and emotions as the human race has?

The blacks had a legend, or ascribed a reason, for all the little ways and tricks of birds and animals. Some of them, too, are very ingenious; some of them pure superstition.

Of the native bear they spoke little. Its humanlike cry awed them. It was "tabu."

They say that at one time the native bear and the fabled bunyip were close friends. Indeed, some averred that the bear is of the bunyip family. It always had the power of becoming invisible.

To prove this they tell of a black who essayed to catch a native bear that had its home in the fork of a big gum-tree somewhere near where the bridge spans the Wollondilly. In spite of the appeals and protestations of his people, he took his waddy and climbed the tree. He reached the bear, and just as he was about to club it the tree opened. The centre was rotted away, and into the hollow the man fell. His cries could be plainly heard outside, but no one dared to do anything to effect a rescue. He was left to slowly weaken and to go out in death.

Though this tale was told many times by the blacks, of course no white man credited it until somewhere in the seventies, when the tree was blown down. Then the bones of the aborigine were found in the trunk. There was no opening from the outside at the bottom of the tree. The bones were of great age.

The story says that the bunyip lived in the Wollondilly and a koala that lived near was on the best of terms with him. The koala's home was on the top of a mountain, and the bunyip made almost nightly excursions from the river at the foot, to sit with the koala and talk of ancient times. Many an aborigine had been almost seared to death by meeting the prowling bunyip.

When it was discovered that the horrible thing always travelled by the one path and frequented the top of the mountain no black would dare to be in the vicinity at night, and no one ever went to the mountain top. It was found that the meetings took place in the very early hours of the mornings, and it was thought for a long time that the bunyip did not leave his hiding place in the day time at all.

No other bear agreed with the friendship that existed between one of their race and a bunyip. The bunyip was hated, but the bears were loved for their gentleness, and their cry, plaintive as it is, reached hearts, and all koalas were safe. The flesh was never eaten.

Now bears argued that should the people find out about the strange friendship their security from molestation would be endangered. And they saw no chance of escape, for they could not travel fast enough. They remonstrated, but the erring bear took no notice. She heeded no warnings. She left her young one unattended while she philandered and meandered with the bunyip.

Then the bears took counsel. They had noticed the mystic markings on the sorcerer of the black men. They had-many of them-often watched the result of this peculiar painting with the clays. In watching they nearly closed their eyes. They pretended to be asleep, for they had seen that many blacks were not allowed to see the rites. The men allowed them to stay because they were "tabu."

All watchful animals, plainly wide awake, such as dingoes, native cats, the larger marsupials, snakes, etc., were all driven off; but the little koalas sitting in a fork, dozing, dozing, were supposed to see nothing.

And they were "tabu."

Yet all the time they were watching and they knew all about it. Therefore the bunyip's companion knew. Nearly all knew. One that was much larger than any other undertook to paint himself and get aid from the spirit that came to the call of the paint and the markings, and when the bear again went up the mountain leaving her young one unprotected the spirit that saw waited for her return. He caused the little one to spring upon the mother's back and to cling there night and day, so that the mother was not free to come and go and to fraternise with the bunyip as before.

The young one clung too tightly; it could not be shaken off.

The mother tried the pipeclay. She only brought the punishment to all the rest of her tribe. Therefore all young bears cling to their mother's back and she is so hampered that she never moves far from the spot where she was born.

And if you look closely into the face of a koala you may see the partially-closed eyes, and the peculiar parting of the hair on its face to correspond with the clay marks.

THE SMILAX

In the Australian bush there is a stiff climbing plant with hard prickles sparsely placed along its entire length, and with broad shining leaves that have little tendrils at their bases. The vine climbs trees and twines itself about shrubs in such a way that it often makes travelling in the bush impossible.

It is named smilax. One variety is without prickles and is known as Smilax glycyphylla. It is also known as Australian Sarsaparilla, and from it our grandmothers (if they were in Australia) brewed a very refreshing drink. Children often chew the leaves of Smilax glycyphylla, and if I remember aright, the taste is at first by no means pleasant, but after a while becomes quite agreeable to the palate.

The aborigines of the Tuggarah Lakes district knew this plant very well, and their story is that a great ancestor was one day pushing his way through a jungle on the bank of a creek and a prickled smilax scraped his shoulder. He did not feel pain at first, but after a while, when the perspiration got into the tiny cuts, he became very angry, believing that he was bewitched. As well as being angry he was frightened. He had a firm belief in a sort of fairy or goblin which he knew as a "wullundigong," which signifies a "little man of the bush!"

He stopped at the foot of a big tree, and peered up amongst its branches and leaves to see if he could detect any of these little men. He did not wait long, for he was not at all certain that the wullundigong, if he were there and saw him looking, would not be able to do him a very great harm. He saw none, of course, but he did see the smilax with the prickles climbing all over a clump of Lilly-pillies just in front of him, and making a thick, dark arbor. To be sure that there were no little men in there he pushed into the place, and of course the little thorns of the smilax scratched him again, and the pain was in the cuts at once.

Then he knew what was the matter. He knew that there were not any wullundigongs troubling him at all, but that there was a plant just as bad and not able to fight. He wished that there were no such plants and he wondered what he could do to rid the land of them.

He had recourse to the clay, in the virtues of which the blacks had such faith. He was not a sorcerer, but he had been allowed to attend the corroborees that were the schools at which sorcerers were taught much of their arts. A great deal of the power of a sorcerer was not the result of any teaching. The markings were. The incantations were. The reasons for there being any sorcerers were. But much more was the invention of each individual humbug, and he generally hid himself for a time while he thought out his ways of frightening the rest. That made a real sorcerer. This man had not done that. He simply had seen that part of the profession that was taught, and he believed in it all.

When he was properly marked he muttered the incantations and waited for a result. That came only in the form of a thought.

He touched some of the glabrous leaves of the offending plant. He slowly passed his fingers along the whole length of the vine.

The prickles disappeared. The leaves changed. They became smaller. He was emboldened and he tried its taste. He found that to be to his liking. He took some to the great people of his tribe and they tasted them and found them to be as he had said. No one was forbidden to eat of the smilax, and everyone from that time took just as he pleased. In that way it was thought the plant would eventually pass out of existence. But the man did not reckon on the fact that he did not touch all, nor did he remember that no article of diet was utterly destroyed. The totem system prevented that. When no foodstuff was eaten by every one (by that wise decree that had been handed down through the ages, but was reserved for those only whose totem it was not, and when that decree was attended with dire pains and magical penalties), then no foodstuff could be entirely eliminated.

So we still have the smilax, one variety without prickles and the other, which some people call "lawyer vine" though there are other "lawyer vines," still with them.

A STAR LEGEND

The group of stars known to us as the Pleiades gave food for much thought to the aborigines. There are several legends surrounding these heavenly bodies. One is that the Kamilaroys of the North Coast were at enmity with those of the mountains, and a messenger had been sent from group to group with the message-stick calling a council to discuss measures for the protection of the camps. But the messenger had become enamoured of a young woman of one of the groups he had visited, and his affection was returned. However, she proved to be of the same totem, and a marriage was forbidden. Both the young people were very sad, and the man pleaded with the head-man, but all for nothing. He was advised to return to his own people.

Then, like so many other disappointed lovers, he grew resentful, and at last determined to be revenged, and even then, if possible, to secure the lady of his choice.

So he went away to the enemies of the group, and conspired with them to show them the "pukkan" by which they might steal unseen to the camps of the coast lands. This track belonged to the priest, and led to a sacred spot where the Great Spirit could be communed with by the priest.

Now, the first thing was to drive the people together, or by some subtle means persuade them to congregate on the one place. This was not an easy thing to do. The people were widely separated during the day, for some were in the bush engaged in hunting there or in obtaining those things from it that were needed to fashion all the implements incidental to camp life, others were still in the camp; many were down on the beach either playing there or searching for food, and the whereabouts of still more were always uncertain, for they were roamers.

Many consultations were held; many plans were formulated; many tricks were explained; but at last it was decided that the messenger return to that group and pretend to have given up all thought of marrying the coveted girl.

When he was back he sought the confidence of the headman and soon was received without suspicion. Then one day, having prepared and found a chance, he set fire to the bush. He had laid good plans for he knew just where to find the girl. He had seen to it that she was persuaded to go out of the way to get something that she wanted. It was to the pukkan that led to the sacred place. When the fire raged towards them they ran right on to the holy of holies. The only other people who saw them were women who were led by the guardians of young girls. These guardians were watching the girl wanted by the messenger. Now they were all frightened and they all rushed to the clearing. This invasion by women into such a place was against all commandments, and evil was bound to follow.

Heaps of clay left by the priest were seen, and all commenced to smear themselves with it without knowing how to do it properly. They thought it would surely preserve them.

They were changed into witchetty grubs. They found holes in a moist and rotten log into which, as is the habit of witchetty grubs, they crept. They were shrunken into very small beings compared with the beings they once were.

The fire came on and on. People ran in all directions and many were destroyed.

Then by the treachery of the messenger the men of the hills came down and they fell upon the rest and the beach group were nearly all killed. Only the denseness of the smoke prevented more of the mountain people from coming down, and those that did come were glad to hasten away to escape it.

Of those that were not killed there was a priest who went to the sacred spot as soon as he could. He sat on the moist and rotten log and mourned for a long time. Then growing hungry he searched for witchetty grubs, for he knew that the log was a favourite place for them. He found first the woman who was the first one to change. He knew that group to be different from those he had seen before and he suspected witchery. He uttered an incantation and the others were brought back to their old form. But they were bewitched. They sought to escape. The lovers cried out to a spirit and the Milky Way was let down from heaven, up which they might travel. All the women went with them and they got to the top; there they halted, forming the Pleiades.

But the man was punished. He could not stay with the woman.

He retired some distance off, and there he stands ever since a lonely looking star which we call Aldebaran.

A BIRD LEGEND

The aborigines sometimes kept birds and animals as pets, but in all instances that may be enquired into it is found that the pet by some mischance or peculiar trait or impulse strayed into a camp and stayed there. However, this had nothing to do with the belief in an "affinity." Nor yet the belief in and recognition of a "totem." That possibly originated in a knowledge of evolution-in the settled idea that during the ages everything has changed in form-and no outstanding fact of Nature escaped being considered the beginning or the dwelling-place of an ancestor or an originator.

But something of a parody of this fundamental belief is the acceptance of an affinity in the shape of a bird or an animal that knows of its being related to a human and who acts as a protector of those of whom it is a family part. In this way the last full-blooded woman of the Cammaray people believed in the snake. She says that the black snake always indicates to her whether or not an undertaking of hers is to be successful, when a calamity is about to happen or has just happened in her immediate family, when she is personally threatened with great loss and whether or not the time be propitious for the doing of any important thing.

She tells many weird tales of warnings shown to her by her affinity. The lyre-bird, she tells, was the affinity of a man of her people away back in the time before history, and he had one as a pet. He was very proud of the fact that his bird mimicked so marvellously, and he arranged a competition. People who belonged to such birds as parrots, black cockatoos, wattle birds-those with a clear, distinctive call-assembled, and they listened to the lyre-bird not only imitating, but excelling each in its own song.

One bird was not claimed by anybody, and it sat disconsolately on a limb, apparently taking no notice of the proceedings; and then, just before dark, it made its effort.

The lyre-bird, nothing loth, imitated it perfectly. But the other bird was not finished. In another key it performed again, and still in

122

another, until the lyre-bird was bewildered. It failed to follow; therefore we may now hear the great bird mimic as we stand, say, at Echo Point in the Blue Mountains, or under the hills of the Snowy or the Cann, going through all its repertoire, imitating not only every other bird, but every sound it has ever heard. But when it comes to the laugh of one it fails. The bird it cannot properly mock is the kookaburra. The lyre-bird man of the story was discredited, and therefore in later years such men were never of much account in the eyes of their compatriots, while those of the kookaburra, though it is recognised as an affinity of a much later date, are always people of great importance.

And by some strange coincidence we have taken the kookaburra to our hearts, and we picture him much more as the bird-representative of Australia than the emu which figures as such officially.

TWO WARATAH LEGENDS

There are many legends concerning the waratah—Australia's most glorious flower and all her own, for it does not occur in any other part of the world, while its supposed rival, the wattle, is as common in all parts of the Southern Hemisphere as it is in Australia. The aborigines wove some very pretty and fanciful stories about their prettiest bloom. Most of them come from the Burragorang Valley, though at least one must have filtered through from very far west, for in this story lies enclosed the fact that the waratah did in early tertiary times flourish in West Australia.

This story is one of the making of the waratah red. It was supposed, it seems, that it was at first a white flower, though that idea does not pervade the other stories of it. Still it was loved then just as much as it is now, and its whiteness did not detract from its charm. The day was away back in the alcheringa and it had been very still and very hot, and the whole tribe, with the exception of one man, lay amongst the bracken in the shade of big eucalypti and lesser myrtles and other scrub. The sweet-scented Sassafras grew there, too, and that other perfumed shrub, the Olearia or Musk, and without a doubt, the exquisite Ceratopetalum or Christmas Bush, as well. The spot was at the foot of very high bouldered cliffs that bounded a deep, clear-pooled river, and the one man who was not prostrated was fishing. All this was in a valley, and out from it the land was a parched and barren tract. The sun blazed down and the heat dazzled, and the sandy and gravelled ground was too hot to walk upon. Now not a zephyr moved the air. The season must have been spring, for the waratah blooms only in that season, always waiting until the cold of winter had retreated to the Pole to which it belongs, or to the regions above the clouds.

Most of the people were asleep. They had retired to the shade. They knew that great cumulus clouds would at length appear from beyond the west and that most surely they would bring thunder and lightning and rain and coolness. An infant-a very pretty child not

124

yet able to walk and perhaps not yet entirely black, for aboriginal babies were born brown, and the black of them showed first under their fingernails and spread from there—crawled away from its dozing mother or whatever woman had charge of it, and the dogs were too indolent in the heat to notice it laboriously getting closer and closer to a tangle of Hibbertia, or Guinea-flower vine, through which stood the Waratah plant resplendent with gleaming white flowers. In there, coiled but alert, lay something else that gleamed-a watching black snake.

Now, the child was of the black snake totem, and, that being so, the reptile was its guardian, not its enemy.

As some of our children have done, the little baby put out its hand to play with the usually deadly thing, and just at that moment the guardian awoke. She missed the child at once. One hurried glance around and she saw the situation. There was the baby about to play with a venomous snake. Forgetting that the child was of that totem and that it would do her no harm, she grabbed a nullah and flung it with all her might, and the back of the snake was broken, and its blood streamed out. The only movement it was then capable of was a swaying of the forward part, and this part it placed around the baby.

Another missile was thrown, and, had the snake not been where it was, the child would certainly have received the blow and been hurt. The snake was again hit, as it, being the protector of the child, intended that it should. Slowly and painfully it unwound itself. The now frightened baby rolled away. The snake laid its injured self amongst the stalks of the waratah bush, and slowly its blood was absorbed as it trickled from the wounds. In a few days streaks of red were to be seen in the flowers, and by degrees the whole of them were so coloured, and therefore we have the bright and beautiful blooms of far greater quantity than the white ones.

It is certainly strange that the white waratahs appear to be much older than the usual crimson ones.

The last full-blooded woman of the Cammaray tribe says that she is a black snake woman and that the black snake is her guardian. When a baby, her life was saved in a manner somewhat similar to the way the baby of this story was saved and it always warns her of approaching danger, and when her intentions, if carried out, will not be to her advantage. So sure is she of that, that she takes careful notice in summer, and she only undertakes serious matters in that season so that she may be warned by her black snake.

ANOTHER LEGEND

One still, hot day in the alcheringa, the people of a tribe that inhabited the same part of Australia as those written of in the preceding story were so prostrated with the intense heat as to be unable to eat. They lay in whatever of shade they could find and awaited the thunderstorm that sometimes came on such days and proved their salvation. Without such coolings of the air very few people could survive. The trees and shrubs were wilting. Eucalypti turned their leaf-edges to the sun to save the blades. Other leaves grew limp. Whatever else of vegetation was there showed the baleful effects of the extreme temperature. A rocky gully had the waratah, and it, too, was as discomfited as the rest of the scanty flora.

But no great cumulus clouds rolled up from the west, and the night fell upon a tired earth and a tired vegetation, and a tired people. No one could sleep. There were mosquitoes to prevent sleep, even if their weariness would send them into slumber. The little children were fretful, and the dogs occasionally hitched themselves closer to some person as if they got a little comfort from such companionship. The sun had gone over the horizon a red ball, and flaming streaks seemed to betoken another day of furnace-like heat to be ready to follow.

Then the sky moved.

In the darkness, with just a shred of the red of the burning west left, and with the stars showing brightly, and a rising moon putting an inquisitive edge over the haze of the east, the sky heaved and billowed arid tumbled and tottered. The moon rocked. The stars tumbled and clattered and fell one against the other. The Milky Way-the "pukkan" or track up which departed spirits often reached the world to which they went-also billowed and it split, and in some places is never joined together again, leaving blank spaces that we call "Magellan's Clouds." These "clouds" to the aborigines are pitfalls set to trap the unworthy spirit travellers, and are also places through which spirits may drop back to earth to assist relatives, or to return in human form.

The great star-groups were scattered, and many of them, loosened from their holds, came flashing to the earth. They were heralded by a huge mass, red and glowing, that added to the number of falling stars by bursting with a deafening roar and scattering in a million pieces which were molten.

The people were too seared to move. The disturbance continued all night. When the smoke and the clamour had died away and morning had dawned it was seen that the holes had been burnt into the earth, and great mounds were formed by the molten pieces, and many caves were made. The burning was still going on, for molten masses and flame were being belched forth.

Certain of the plants received the red pieces of the bursting masses, and they are the red flowering ones. The Waratah is one of them.

MIST AND A FRINGE FLOWER

It is said that many departed aborigines return to this earth in human form. A legend has already been written in which is the thought that blackfellows often slipped during their journey along the Milky Way through Magellan's Clouds, and came back here. Dense mists were supposed to envelop these returning people, for they were too considerate to make themselves visible suddenly and thus frighten their relatives. They remembered how frightened they themselves had been always when any not-understood phenomenon took place, and they took care not to willingly cause such consternation now that they were from the other world. Yet by inadvertence this was often done.

Aborigines were generally much frightened when mists came, and they often crouched in the shelter of crevasse or camp until they had cleared away. They feared the unseen, and they could not conjecture what fearsome thing might be hidden. They watched the curling, eddying vapour, and their imaginative and often artistic minds saw many fleeting shapes. There is a story of fire coming with a mist which is called "pouraller," and burnt stones near Appin were pointed out as a place where this particular mist often covered the country. No doubt the fact that volcanoes emitted fire with steam is responsible for this idea which has become somewhat distorted in its passage down the ages since Canobolas in New South Wales and Mount Fairy in Victoria and Mounts Gambier and Schanck in South Australia threw out their molten masses.

The strip of country between the Appin Creek and George's River was the home of a very powerf ul group. To-day the watershed drained by the Cataract and the Loddon rivers is one source of Sydney's Water Supply. The head of George's River is in the same locality, but it falls the opposite way and its waters do not flow into the Cataract Dam. On it are King's Falls; on the Loddon the Loddon Falls; on the other creek the Appin Falls. All are most picturesque, though the Appin Falls are now quite governed by the floodgates of the Dam. The real owners of this country roamed over the luxuriant forest. In our time the village of Sherbrooke was built there and Frank Knight's sawmill is responsible for the destruction of the beautiful woods. The natives travelled the peaty patch known to us as Madden's Plains in the days of their mastery, and from the edge of the Illawarra Range they saw the sight that we recognise as the most beautiful in the whole world. When they roamed towards the setting sun they went as far as the Nepean, which winds itself along the foot of the hills of the Blue Mountains.

Madden's Plains is the country of many mists. It was somewhere there that a pretty purple flower grew, and it was there that an old man died—an old man of story and of truth.

Before his burial his womenfolk sat in a little circle and manifested their grief. A son passed by in jaunty fashion just as if he did not care, and the old women ceased their lamentations and cornmenced upbraiding him in loud, angry, querulous voices. He answered them back, and it seemed as if a quarrel, bitter and vociferous, must ensue. Two other young men took sides with their comrade, and the whole camp would have been involved had not the undertakers come to bear away the body to its resting-place.

The spirit had gone. The Milky Way seemed to be closer than usual, and in the morning the whole county was enveloped in a thick mist. It swung up from the jungle at the foot of the range and swept by over the plains and the creeks and the scrub, and must have been lost in the clouds that surely hovered on the crests of the Blue Mountains.

No one stirred from the camp. But the women had not spent their desire to scold the man whom they knew was too callous to feel the death of his father. And he, of all the people, ventured forth into the mist. He had had enough of the tongues of the old mourners.

He had plucked a little stalk that bore several of the pretty violet flowers, and for want of something better to do, or in order to soothe his ruffled feelings, he sat beside a log and quietly and deftly tore the edge of the petals, making them nicely fringed.

Slowly the mist rolled away, and in its billowings was to be seen the form of a man. A short distance off he appeared again, only to be once more swallowed up in another wave. By this time the sorrowing women saw him and in frightened whispers they told the people. Then break after break occurred in the driven mist, and gradually the sun came through it. A short time after it had gathered itself together and had gone away, and the country was clear and crisp and damp, and the sunlight was warm. And slowly approaching from up the creek that we call Muddy Creek was a man. He had the form and the voice of the one for whom the women were grieving. His hands he carried behind his back.

Without a word he strode slowly to the young man, who still sat tearing the violet flowers. Of all the people he was the only one who was blind to the visitor. It was not given to him to see a spirit-man, just as it is not possible for white people to see what can be seen by the natives. Suddenly the hands came from behind the back and a nullah was swung down upon the head of the youth. Because the flower had three petals the spirit-man struck that many blows. There were three marks on the youth's head. The flower fell to the ground, and because it was damp and warm the seeds soon germinated and the resultant flowers had fringed petals. It is a lily. We know it as Thysanotus or Fringed Violet. Perhaps it is a pity it was ever called a violet. It is said by the blacks that it only opens in a mist, and that before the mist clears away the spirit of the slain youth has to tear every petal and make them fringed. The three blows are perpetuated in the wale or bruise-like mark on every petal. It is strange, surely, that so gruesome a story should have been told about such a delicate and beautiful flower.

There is a rather pretty story about the fringed gum-blossom, and in it is a reference to a sea and an island in the centre of Australia.

MULGANI

This is a true tale about some black people who lived in this country before any white people set foot in it—long before.

Unlike the other stories which are legends that have actually been told as legends, this was not told regarding one specific happening nor one particularised person nor persons. It was done by many. It may be called a type story. Just what is said the people thought was really thought by many, and just what is said the imagined people did was really done by many.

In that way it is brought before readers what was thought and what was done, though Mulgani is created to bring it all.

Read first what a tribe was. It was a very large number of people who were broken up into many groups, big and little. These groups thought themselves a family, and the names they had were family names. We whites call just a father and mother and their children a family. The aborigines considered that all children belonged as much to all the uncles and aunts and cousins as to the actual father and mother, and uncles and aunts were those men and women whose brothers and sisters the actual father and mother might have married, seeing that they belonged to the proper totems. So their idea of family was much wider than ours.

Mulgani was a pretty little aboriginal baby. She was born hundreds and hundreds of years ago.

Let me now tell you how to speak of the black people. You should say "aborigine" when you mean a person, but "aboriginal" when you mean the kind of person. For the bigger people who read this book I will tell that the word "aborigine" is a noun and the word "aboriginal" is an adjective. Therefore we say that a story (for instance) is an aboriginal story and the first teller of it was an aborigine.

Mulgani was a Katungal. Her people lived away down on the South Coast of New South Wales, at Twofold Bay. An atlas here would be a useful book to have beside you as you read, for in it you can see the names of the places.

Now there was to be a great ceremony at a pretty spot near where is now the Excelsior Coal Mine at Thirroul.

Mulgani's father heard about it. A messenger had arrived at Twofold Bay and he brought with him a piece of stick about a foot long and about an inch in diameter. It was a piece of waratah stem and on it were cut some marks. Some of these marks were just circles cut right round it, and between the circles little cuts were made that looked like four-legged stools. Then again there were spots or dots. The marks were a strange written language, for they could be deciphered by a few men of the people wherever the stick was shown. To be a messenger was no easy task, for before he could have his intentions understood, and before he could reach the readers of whatever tribe or group he wished to visit, he ran the risk of being misunderstood and perhaps speared. Of course he carried weapons with him. But when he came in sight of a camp he waited quietly, generally sitting on a log or on the ground. Then when he was seen he threw his spears to the ground. After being received he was allowed to go back and recover the spears. No one of the visited people were ever known to steal such spears. It is known, though, that messengers have been killed by mistake or mischance or for some serious reason and their weapons remained where they were laid down, and were found there long years afterwards.

Mulgani was only a few weeks old. She was not yet even black. She was a dark brown colour, but the real black that commenced under her fingernails was spreading, and soon she would be as black as any aborigine could be.

Her father and mother were watching her very closely, for they were anxious, not wishing her to be too long becoming as black as they were. She had been, as was usual, kept covered with fat-the fat of the wombat if such animals were native to the district-and powdered charcoal. Her aunts saw to that, and it was done for two reasons: first that she might appear black, and secondly that she might be put out in the sun and burnt by it without it hurting her tender skin. The wind, too, would have chapped her, but the covering prevented it.

Now her father was very fond of flowers. He had made many trips to the mountains that lie away to the west of Twofold Bay-the Muniong Range we call them-and he had seen all the trees and shrubs and plants of the bush. He had picked some and had brought them back to Mulgani's mother before Mulgani was born, and the mother wished that she could go to the mountains and get some for herself.

And now this messenger had come with the message-stick to tell the Karungals about the big ceremony, and although Mulgani was only a few days old, the father and mother intended to go to it.

But the father had to attend a night school for a few nights.

He had not ever been taught how to prepare Styphelia berries or Geebungs (called Persoonia by the botanists) and Astrolomas or Ground berries. These berries were often eaten raw, but because Mulgani's father had been told that he must not eat them unless they were cooked he had never eaten them at all. He got quite enough of other foods that were not forbidden him. Of course they were mostly cooked too. Now that he was with many others going on a very long journey, taking his wife and little child, it was considered that there might be some difficulty in obtaining enough food, therefore no article must be neglected, and there were certain ways for all the people to live, and those ways were taught them at the proper corroborees. If they were not treated correctly there was the danger of magic being in them. Of course we can see that the magic was only the poison that so many fruits have, and which is nullified by some sort of preparation. This idea of magic was not of a lot of primitive people with no sense nor reason at all. The people were primitive, but they had sense and knowledge, and there is a basis for every thought and every custom. No doubt some time away back in the ages a blackfellow was made sick by eating the green geebung, and that happening was ascribed simply to magic. We must not belittle a blackfellow because he speaks of magic. Why, see this:-Only a little while ago I heard a woman-a white woman-say that waratahs should riot be kept in a house because they brought bad luck. What is that but blackfellow's magic. And for no reason at all. No one ever became unlucky, no one ever died, or was made sick, by the waratah. There is no basis for the idea. Then that white woman was far more ignorant than the blacks in that respect. That some flowers do make us sick is well known. If we do not call the reason magic, then it is because we have found out that it is the superabundance of pollen that is the cause of the sickness. The wattle flower is one of those in which there is danger because of its great quantity of pollen.

Anyhow tiny Mulgani's father was very anxious to go to the school, and he was very pleased when he found that the king had ordered such a school to be held. Everybody of the group that lived around Twofold Bay could attend.

Many schools were secret, and only the teachers and the special scholars and those who had already been to such schools were allowed to be present. Such schools were those at which things were

133

taught and ceremonies were enacted that might be described as sacred. And all schools were termed by white people "corroborees," and for a long time they were thought to be nothing more than dances. There were dances, too, and they also are called corroborees.

After the school those who were to travel to the great ceremony set out.

The way was long and in places difficult. Mulgani was often carried by one or other of her aunts.

Sometimes the party was right on the beach, sometimes on the sandhills and sometimes in the scrub. But never did they go too far from the sight and the sound of the waves. On the sand-hills there were very pretty flowers-the Mesembryanthemum, a very brilliant and dainty vine and just at the bases the big yellow Hibbertia, and gleaming purple masses of Hardenbergia.

The Malelucas were in blossom and the sweet scent that they give out was a great pleasure to the travellers, though of course Mulgani was far too young to notice such a thing as that.

They came to the Shoalhaven River. The party travelled up it on the high rocky sides for many miles. Then they came across a camp of people of their own tribe, but of course a different group. Here they were welcomed and given the best of food. It was better than any they had got since starting out.

While they rested in this camp Mulgani's father went out and gathered the Styphelia berries and the Astrolomas, and what he did not cook he put in the dilly bag that was carried by his wife. It was delightful to see how the wallabies were cooked and how the best parts were given to those who should by right of birth or age have them.

The travellers stayed there for about a week, and during that time every day Mulgani was put on the ground out in the sun. She was quite happy, and her father and mother showed with pride that she was now all black.

Many of the people of this group joined the travellers. They had heard of the intended ceremony and the summons and were awaiting the coming of this party.

Soon they came to the country of the tall, swaying cabbage-palms and the staghorns and the treeferns. Many of the big detached rocks had the dendrobiums with their long creamy fronds of flowers, and the sweet scent was better by far than that of the tea-trees they had passed through, for the flower of the Dendrobium speciosum is more sweetly scented than almost any other in our Australian bush. There is, however, one other that must be mentioned here, though

134

the travellers did not see it. It is the Symphyonema paludosum. It grows only in swampy places, and such swamps do not occur anywhere along the route taken, though they are not very far away for they are on the top of the range under which the ceremony took place.

In another week the party reached the spot and they found a big gathering of people. Some had come from over the range.

There were fires and smoke and feasting and singing and the beating of drums. There were corroborees, some of them, such as dances, for the whole of the gathering; and there were also those secret ones for only the special people.

Mulgani was a toddler before she was brought back to her own country.

THE LEGEND OF THE PLEIADES

Amongst the Mungulkabultu group of the great Chepara tribe of Queensland there was once a king who ruled most severely over his people, but who was extraordinarily lenient with those of any neighbouring tribe or group.

There was a time when all the groups were so very friendly as to make the whole tribe accessible to one another, but the discipline was such that there could be no undue fraternising and no trespasses. But now there was a laxness. People of the forbidden totems were received into each group, and forbidden marriages became somewhat common.

Yunguipan was the son of Paira the king, and he was an emu man.

He, according to the age-old laws should not have been permitted to look at an emu woman. We can see the wisdom of this rule.

Wakolo was the daughter of Kari, and Kari was also an emu woman.

Wakolo was about thirteen years of age and her sister had gone over to the camp of the marriageable maidens and the widows.

A great tribal fight had just taken place. The "pukkan" that led from the top of the mountain right down to the coast wound in places between great rocks, and was so overgrown in others that it was easy to leave it and wander far amongst the great towering Stenocarpus trees, and the eucalypti, and the ferns, before the traveller discovered that he was wrong.

Several men of the coast group had wandered lost in the jungle, and some had been speared by the Mungulkabultu people.

Then came a threat brought by a messenger with a message-stick, and it was answered by jeers.

The Mungulkabultus demanded many things of the men of the mountain and included in them was the girl Wakolo.

The coast people were of the same tribe as those of the mountain,

136

but of a group that should have no dealings with them. Still they bore the same name.

Perhaps there would have been no trouble had the disciplining been as strict as it should have been.

Then after a time, there being no lasting decision in consequence of the fight, another king who was a strict king, ruled over the mountain people and he insisted that no more marriages take place between the groups except under special circumstances, and he was obeyed. In time they came to consider themselves a different people and they called themselves the Riste-burras. And another messenger picked his way amongst the thick undergrowth and the fallen brambles and between the giant trunks of gum-trees and the stems of palms. He was from the Riste-burras of the mountain and he came to the Mungulkabultus of the coast. Wakolo watched. She knew of that message and those demands of some years ago, and as yet she was not married.

This new messenger carried also demands. Wakolo was not specially mentioned, but women were demanded, and she thought that she would have to leave her people if there was a fight and her men were defeated. The Coast people were victorious and they returned to their lands carrying spoil and driving women before them. Wakolo was not amongst them. She returned to her camp and she found it broken and the women scattered about in the bush and the men standing apart.

Amongst them was Yunguipan. Paira the king was dead.

Suddenly Yunguipan spoke. He gave orders regarding the burial of his father and the disposal of his widows, and he ordered a march to another ridge and a camp to be fixed there. In this new camp Wakolo's sister went to the wurlies of the widows and those maidens that chose that place.

Yunguipan watched her go.

As was the custom several young men visited this camp in the evening, but not until some weeks had passed away since its formation.

Then the sister of Wakolo found a young man standing close to her wurlie, and as soon as she looked into his eyes be asked the question of a suitor.

"What do you eat, my girl?"

This question was put to find out for a certainty whether or not the two were of different totems and the suit might therefore be continued.

But it will be remembered that it was not a long time since the careless king had allowed the laxity.

Often an emu man of the now Riste-burras had been allowed to woo and win and take an emu girl, not only of the Mungulkabultus but even of the Riste-burras.

Wakolo's sister and the young man had spent some hours talking, and at several of the other wurlies, including some of the widows, were other young men talking in low tones.

And to this camp came, too, the young king.

He also looked at Wakolo's sister. He and Yunguipan often went to the same place.

One night as they sat talking Wakolo came up and without a word she entered the wurlie of her sister. The young king followed her in.

That night one of the old wise men-a councillor and a priest of the group-visited the king in his own camp. He instructed him in many things pertaining to the marriage rules and the married state. He told him that it was certainly wrong for an emu man to marry an emu woman, and he gave instances of the transgression of this law resulting in much harm to the whole tribe, and of course he ascribed the happening to magic.

It had no effect. Yunguipan still continued to visit Wakolo and her sister in the camp of the maidens.

Down on the coast the group were satisfied with that victory of many months before, and they were very quiet.

Now the priest who had advised the young king was very wroth upon seeing that his warnings had been disregarded, and he secretly visited the camp of the Riste-burras. He went as a messenger, pretending that he had a message from his king to the effect that a great ceremony was to be enacted-the ceremony of the initiation of the young men.

But as he went from group to group showing his false message-stick he always found someone to whom he said that the young king of his group was breaking the marriage rules and that his transgressions would certainly result in some great disaster befalling the whole tribe now called the Chepara Tribe, and he advised the bringing of weapons to some secret place near the camp of the Mungulkabultus.

And so it was done, and the false messenger returned to his own people.

While the king was courting the sisters, Wakolo, and the other, the neighbouring groups were preparing, some to avenge the wrong done to the ancestors by young Yunguipan, and some in the belief that a special ceremony was to be performed to which they were invited as a very great favour.

But the false messenger had made one great mistake. He had listened in the Riste-burra group to a tale of woe told him by one captive woman, and her husband knew of it.

Therefore when all was ready for the attack upon the Mungulkabultus this man ran ahead and found Yunguipan.

He quickly told him of the treachery of the priest.

Yunguipan was both angry and afraid. He ran to the father of the girls and told him what he had heard. Kari, the mother, heard the tale, and she counselled her husband to advise the king to go to the place where the sacred rites of the men were performed, and there, perhaps, to find advice and a way out. She herself had never seen this place, but she fully believed that from it men returned with vigour and wisdom. Yunguipan believed this advice to be best.

Down amongst the tribes near the coast the preparations for a journey to the country of the Mungulkabultus were being hurried. The other people had been warned by the false messenger and were already marching to the country of the Riste-burras, or had gathered there. There was unusual secrecy about it all, for many men had sneaked away and had hidden weapons at places near the "pukkan."

When the day came it was very, very hot. The sun poured its dry rays out of a leaden sky, and the rocks of the sparsely-clad mountain side shed the intensified heat.

But down in the gullies the verdure was thick, and in a cool spot there, not far from the track, was the sacred spot that no woman was permitted to look upon.

Thither sped Yunguipan.

The false messenger had done his work well. Those people who believed that they were travelling to a big initiation ceremony were surprised to see a large number of men suddenly appear amongst them with all their weapons, and marking one another with the red ochre of war as they walked.

Soon the fury broke loose. Yunguipan was in the sacred grove. He heard the yells. He had just received communication from the spirits of his ancestors and he rushed to the camp of the widows and maidens. Wakolo and her sister he spied first. Throwing his cloak over them he picked them up in his arms and bore them away, and many others from that camp followed.

In his hurry and his excitement Yunguipan rushed without thinking of possible danger, to the sacred place. He reached it and found that he and the sisters were surrounded by others of the maidens' camp-both maidens and widows.

And now he realised that he had made a very great mistake. What would happen now?

He again called upon the spirits of his ancestors and his prayer was answered. He asked that he might be given something by which he could save the lives of himself and the sisters, and as he could riot kill any of the others who came into the sacred place if he also did not kill Wakolo, he asked that they might be saved too.

The sounds of fighting came nearer. Several men of the Riste-burras came rushing through the bushes, and Yunguipan knew that they were being defeated. It was too dangerous for him to return to his people-more dangerous even than to be seen by the enemy. So he crept into a hollow log, taking several women with him, for there was not room for them all. The others found hollow logs also. There was room for all now.

Then the magical thing happened. Yunguipan felt himself changing. His skin went white and shrank until it was painful, for it was shrinking too fast for his flesh and bones. He made several incisions with the yam-stick of Wakolo around himself, and the surplus flesh and bones came out.

Bood fell upon the women and they had to do similarly, and at last each became a little white grub.

One of the other women came to the log of Yunguipan, and she too was stained with the blood, and when she returned she contaminated all the rest.

So the whole party became grubs, and in one log were Yunguipan and seven women, while how many of the others there were no one knows.

The men of the coast groups were utterly defeated. The sinning king was absent from the fighting, as I have told, and the rest were able to fight strongly, and before night the invaders of the mountain country were in full retreat, leaving some dead and many sorely wounded.

The victorious Mungulkabultus followed down the track and they came upon the waiting people, and, flushed as they were, they fell upon them and captured many prisoners whom they killed.

Then they returned and they asked one another what had become of Yunguipan and the women from the camp of the maidens.

No one knew.

They also asked why they had been attacked. The false messenger stood in fear and trembling. His agitation was noticed, and suspicion fell upon him, and to escape for the while he went down to the sacred place. He saw there many signs that it had been visted by many people. He saw, too, the yam-sticks lying about. So he sat on a log-the very log in which Yunguipan and his seven followers had taken refuge and were now housed as white grubs all wrinkled over, and he wondered what he was to do and how he might escape the wrath that he knew was so likely to fall upon him.

Then another misfortune befell the people. The side of the mountain burst into flames.

Perhaps the hot sun shining down through the dry air so heated the mica or some other mineral in the rock that it set fire to a tiny wisp of moss or flower or grass and there was just enough breeze to fan it into flame.

From such tiny beginnings many conflagrations have been known to grow into huge destructive forest fires that have destroyed thousands of acres of good bush country and grass lands. The fire came down the mountain as rapidly as a waterfall comes over the rocks, and it swept into the gullies and mounted the tops of tall trees. It sent the heated and expanded air driving up into the heavens, and as the lower air rushed to the space thus caused about the flame a gale was made that drove the fire hither and thither leaving no spot unburned.

An advancing wave of flame sped to the camp.

The blacks ran to the nearest watercourse.

The man on the log at the sacred place saw the fire coming to him.

He was fairly safe, for the place was clear. Only a few very big logs lay about, and in two of them were the strange magic grubs.

The heat became terrific. Yunguipan and the women felt it and they began to wriggle and squirm. The man heard them, and in spite of his danger and in spite of the heat he probed into the log with one of the yam-sticks.

He found Wakolo and she uttered a scream. Immediately Yunguipan came out of his hole and he seized the hand that held the stick.

The fire died down.

Those who escaped it returned to the place of the camp.

New wurlies had to be built, but there was no place where young widows and maidens segregated themselves as was usual.

That there were many grubs in the logs of the sacred place was told by the priest who had hidden there, and permission was given to certain woman to go there and probe for them. This was another transgression of rules. Yunguipan came out from his log and he called to the others.

Wakolo was badly wounded. So Yunguipan spun two nets, into

which he gathered all the women—himself and seven in one net, and the rest in another-and when the moon was full and it sent a long beam like a strip of carpet right down to the sacred place, with their legs through the meshes the two netfuls of grubs walked up and up until they reached the sky. The women down below probed the holes in the logs in vain, for there were no grubs to be got.

Bathing in the seas of the moon, Yunguipan and the women became stars, and they had to find a place amongst the other stars in the sky. They crossed the Milky Way, that pukkan of the departed spirits upon which they travel from the earth to heaven, and after wandering for many years they at last settled down.

Yunguipan is now Aldebaran, and the seven maidens are the visible Pleiades. One that seems to be broken is the wounded Wakolo. The other women are there, too, and they are the invisible members of the same group of stars. They are faintly visible when the night is clear with frost and there is no haze anywhere. The net can still be distinguished, and there is a long thread that connects the group of Aldebaran.

This story of the Pleiades is known, with just a little variation, to nearly all the tribes of Queensland, and even to the Kamilaroys in New South Wales.

THE BLACK SATIN

On the South Coast of New South Wales (not the Illawarra coast, which is not the South Coast) is a wonderful tract of deeply undulated forest, wild and jungled bush. The highlands of this big territory overhang a strip of well-scrubbed and verdant bush which rolls north and south, showing the creeks and gullies by the deepness of the purple, and which, eastward, thins out to paddocks of perpetual grass with broad waters spread in them, and they in turn slip downward to curved edges and curved broad beaches of gleaming yellow sand broken into scallops by lion-like promontories that gaze out-ever out—over the great blue expanse of Pacific Sea.

These highlands are but foothills, though far-flung, of Australia's Great Dividing Range. They have been pressed to where they are by great weight. It is as though one day they will be pressed on and will cover the jungle and will be engulfed out over the beaches.

The jungle is the home of giant gums and dense myrtle, of umbrageous fig and tall palm, of sassafras and supplejack. The millions of shafted trees rear their topmost boughs up into the clouds and stand as great pillars, and the voice of animal and bird reverberates as the human voice does amongst fluted pillars of a great cathedral. But the movement of wallaby and bandicoot and bushrat, of the lyre-bird as he scratches, of the spotted native eat and the wallaroo, is silent, for there is a carpet of fallen leaves that allows no more sound than does the Axminster or the Brussels of the mansion.

All the wonder growth of our best Australian bush in this piece of country. Gullies are deep and dark. Rolling ridges are rounded and ferned. Down in the depths the creeks lie still. All the ferns, all the mosses, all the deep-green, rank-grown underscrub hem the chill waters of the little sunless creeks and close them about. Trailing vines and heavy myrtles make the gullies almost impenetrable. Up the slope of the mountain the scrub is less, and massed burrawangs hang out their fronds as if to repel the wanderer.

143

In one of the densest of the gullies, where the Eugenias and the Ceratopetalums hide the carpet of fallen leaves, lived a family of satin birds. The King of the Family was jet-black.

Down on the shores of the great wide Casuarina-fringed lagoons lived a family of aborigines. Their king was jet-black, and his totem was the satin bird of like colour. When the hunters tired of fishing, and when they wearied of crossing the sand-dunes and the glaring, shimmering beachglaring and shimmering on every fine day of summer-to poke off the mussels and spear the butterfish and groper, they pushed through the Ceratopetalums and the burrawangs, and, following the tortuous bed of the principal creek amid the ferns and the moss and the vines and the myrtles, gradually ascending, they entered the sub-tropical patch where the ferns were huge and lank and staghorns clustered on rocks and trees, and the beautiful Dendrobium clung, and the supplejacks and leatherwoods and bangalow palms ran up in slender height, and that pretty massive parasite-the wild fig-made its umbrageous shade, as has been written. Here they rested.

No shaft of sunlight ever penetrated through this dense foliage. Never did the fallen nor clinging plants here feel drying wind or see a sunbeam. It was never dry.

The porcupine pushed his spikey body through, slowly raising and lowering his banded quills, and the fat bandicoot snouted for roots, and sleek tiger-cats lay in wait for the pretty green tree-snake, and for other venomous reptiles; the brown-banded and carpet and diamond snakes twined among the vines or lay coiled between the damply warm roots.

Above, in the upper branches, the colonies of pretty flock and top-knot pigeons clattered, and a little lower the parrots and gill-birds shrieked. Below them the wrens and tits mingled with fantails' both black and brown, and down on the ground the little seed-eaters darted, while the coy lyre-bird stood and made his mocking calls or scratched powerfully to unearth his meats-the grubs and bugs and roaches of the damp underscrub.

When they had rested enough the straying hunters, with singleness of thought, arose and pushed on and up.

A wall of rock rose sheer with just one narrow cleft down which the water rushed or fell, and on the level crest of that a view above the figs and other tops out over the Ceratopetalums and burrawangs, and across the shimmering surface of the lake above the now hazy sand-dunes and beach to the wide, flat, blue sea, met the admiring gaze of the men.

But there was still far to go.

A wide slope down again to the level at the back of the ridge where the water of the creek was a miniature lake with just the narrow cleft cut through the wall, and down where the vines grew again and the eucalypti were mingled with turpentine.

A few hours' tramping and struggling with impending vines here, and they came to the gully of the satin birds. The darting, timid birds with the shining greenish plumage sat stock still while they watched the party of hunters. The jet-black king had chosen a burnt patch on the side of a Richea, and there he clung, his colour and that of the grass-tree making him almost invisible.

Then one of the hunters spied the home of his favourite grub on the side of this grass-tree, and as he detoured to get it the black satin thought he was discovered and he sprang out. He was very fat and heavy, and the surrounding scrub was thick, so he flapped awkwardly into the entanglement of Clematis and Eugenias.

This was his mistake and proved his undoing. Like a flash the nullah was flung, and with a grunt of satisfaction the aborigine rushed forward and seized his victim.

Now one of the party was the brother of the king of the group, and he, too, was of the satinbird totem. He asked to be allowed to examine the king of the satin birds, and, without touching it, having satisfied himself that it was really the totem of his father and himself, he said that it must not be again produced so that he could see it. The man who killed it must hide it, and it must be cooked and eaten quite out of sight of any man whose totem it was.

The black bird was hidden in the bag that was worn attached to the rope of fur around the black man's waist.

The giant range was still far ahead and there were many miles of this wooded country to be traversed before the party could reach the blue top that met the sky, and they pushed on until it was too dark to go further. No food was eaten that evening, and the dead satin bird remained fully feathered in the bag of the captor.

During the night he rolled in his sleep and the bag was emptied.

The black satin slipped beside the bird man.

In the morning when he awoke he saw what had happened, and because he was a bird man he was very frightened. He had been taught that he must never handle the king of the satin birds. The whole family was to him tabu, but the most tabu was the black one.

People who were tree people or flower people, or indeed of any other totem, could handle the satin bird and eat it.

However, as the custom was, he said nothing. All day he wondered what would be the ill that would come to him.

145

Once, in going over the deep creek by traversing one of the hundred logs that lay from bank to bank-a creek that wound along the foot of the enormous range-he slipped, and a jagged broken limb caused a deep wound in his leg and he thought that that was perhaps the punishment.

After that the real ascent, with all its difficulties and dangers, began. The men were behind a high pointed mass of mountain rocks that held a huge stone poised on its top and they were shut in by that and the surrounding steeps and by a wall of thousands of feet which was yet to be climbed, and then the sun went out.

Unnoticed, the day had changed.

Buried as they were in the dense forest the sky was out of their ken.

It had dulled. Deep clouds had spread over it, and now as they scaled into a higher air they found it to be raw and chill and a wind was blowing with a grim, steady persistence that foreshadowed rain in plenty.

Presently a fierce gust swept along the side, and after that the heavy rain fell. The black men huddled together and were at first undecided about what to do.

Presently it was agreed that the best thing was to return to the shelter of the gully behind the sharp-topped mount, there to await the passing of the rain. They lit fires and the man with the black satin turned his back to the rest to pluck it, and he took fire from the little heap, and out of the sight of the others he cooked his bird.

The son of the king ran no risks. He, too, parted from the group, and did his own cooking and he ate in silence. They all had berries and pieces of wallaby flesh. Only the satin was to any of them a totem thing.

Suddenly there came a roar from the mountain side. Huge boulders were crashing down the steep. A rock had given way, and it came on, bringing others, and felling trees, and the group of blacks were right in its path. They scrambled up and each ran, holding the cooked food in the hands, to escape.

The falling mass was almost upon them. It was coming far more swiftly than any of them could run. Though it was impeded by trees so also were they by the scrub. The wound in the leg of the king's son prevented him from going as fast as the others, and the man with the piece of satin bird in his hand stayed to aid him. He grasped the arm of the other and they sped on, stumbling and falling, but progressing. Then their hands slipped together and each touched the totem.

Then they were paralysed. They fell. A big tree crashed.

146

The rest escaped. They got out of the path of the avalanche of rocks.

When the falling debris was stilled and the rain was ceasing and the wind was lessening they retraced their strides and they found the unlucky pair.

This put an end to their adventure. All knew what was their own totem, of course, and all knew that an outraged ancestor would have a revenge when he saw a disrespect, whether intentional or not. The ancestors were all jealous gods and they found ways of visiting such a sin upon everyone connected with it.

They returned the way they went out. There were the usual lamentations and the usual mourning period. The wives especially were required to show great sorrow, and by painting themselves with white clay, and pulling out their hair, and by cutting themselves in various places, particularly straight down the middle of the head so that blood ran over the face and down the neck, they satisfied the onlookers that they were genuinely grieved. No one ever went exactly to the place of the tragedy. Therefore, when, long years afterwards, white men were clambering about that steep of the great Curockbilly Range, they found the bones, and a derelict remnant of that once virile family told enough for me to write the true story of the black satin.

THE ABORIGINES

I write of those who held this land
From time as far back as you will-
To-day a wasted, stricken band.
But yesterday a stalwart race
Preserving in the gentle face
The imprint of God's fingers still.
Ere Ovid's parchment spread the ink
The tale was legend of the lips Of Perseus.
And so, I think, 'Tis well to teach the world the lore
Our aborigines forebore
To teach-SAVE TO THEMSELVES-AND THEY'RE

NOT QUIPS!

But we who've peeped into their hearts
See there the deep and passioned beat-
We see how quick a teardrop starts-
We read the furrows of the brow.

147

We know the ache that's with them now.
We note their dragging, listless feet.
They count their age since life began
Here, they the embryo at dawn;
Here lived they when the earth was wan!
Their age is aeons-is not years!
And now they're dying of their tears!
Down in their ashes hear them mourn.
They had no sea-borne argosy.
They trecked no treck with questing feet-
Such tales—they are but fantasy!
Their God was Love-their life was law;
Diseaseless, happy! Why wish more?
In purity they had their seat.
Then came white wings that brought them Death.
They'd lived by love—but Nature saw
In tune with God—sweet as His breath-
But now they see who is the Last.
They know their day has faded fast-
We lie-'tis Nature's law!

C. W. Peck

www.ingramcontent.com/pod-product-compliance
Lightning Source LLC
Chambersburg PA
CBHW020455100426
42813CB00031B/3374/J